ROMAN CATHOLIC
CLERICALISM

THREE HISTORICAL STAGES IN THE LEGISLATION
OF A NON-EVANGELICAL, NOW DYSFUNCTIONAL, AND
SOMETIMES PATHOLOGICAL INSTITUTION

Joe Holland

www.joe-holland.net

PACEM IN TERRIS PRESS

Devoted to the memory of Saint John XXIII,
founder of Postmodern Catholic Social Teaching,
and in support of the search for a Postmodern Ecological Civilization
drawing on the ecological-spiritual wisdom traditions
of our global human family.

www.paceminterrispress.com

ISBN-13: 978-0999608883
ISBN-10: 0999608886

(with corrections of 2018-11-14)

Cover image from Shutterstock by Jorisvo.
Sainted-glass window in Saint Gummarus Church in Lier Belgium
depicting the Church Fathers Saints Gregory of Nazianzus,
Athanasius of Alexandria, John Chrysostom, and Basil.

Pacem in Terris Press publishes scholarly books directly or indirectly related to
Catholic Social Teaching and its commitment to justice, peace, ecology, and spirituality,
and on behalf of the search for a Postmodern Ecological Civilization.
In addition, to support ecumenical and interfaith dialogue,
as well as dialogue with other spiritual seekers,
Pacem in Terris Press publishes scholarly books from other Christian perspectives,
from other religious perspectives, and from perspectives of other spiritual seekers,
that promote justice, peace, ecology, and spirituality
for our global human family.

Opinions or claims expressed in publications from Pacem in Terris Press
represent the opinions and claims of the authors and do not necessarily represent
the official position of Pacem in Terris Press, the Pacem in Terris Ecological Initiative,
Pax Romana / Catholic Movement for Intellectual & Cultural Affairs - USA
or its officers, directors, members, or staff.

PACEM IN TERRIS PRESS
is the publishing imprint of

PAX ROMANA
CATHOLIC MOVEMENT FOR INTELLECTUAL & CULTURAL AFFAIRS
USA
1025 Connecticut Avenue NW, Suite 1000,
Washington DC 20036
www.paceminterris.net

Therefore, elders (*presbyterous*) among you,

I, who [am] a co-elder (*sumpresbyteros*)

and witness of the sufferings of the anointed one (*christos*),

and who [am] also a sharer in [the] about-to-be revealed glory,

exhort [you]:

Shepherd the flock of God among you,

overseeing (*episkopountes*) not by constraint,

but voluntarily according to God;

not out of greed but eagerly;

not lording-over (*katakyrieuontes*) the chosen (*kleron*),

but being examples to the flock.

FIRST EPISTLE OF PETER

Chapter 1, Verses 1-3

The above is a literal translation from the Greek text.

All other biblical quotations are from the New American Bible.

TABLE OF CONTENTS

T he clerical sex-abuse and coverup scandals caused by a significant minority of the episcopacy and presbyterate of the Roman
Catholic Church (but one of twenty-four churches in the Global Catholic Communion) has precipitated a strategic intellectual debate between the Church's so-called "progressive" and "conservative" wings.

This small book has not been written to side completely with either
wing of that debate, but rather *to look deeper at the systemic level*. But first
let us briefly review the conservative and progressive diagnoses.

- The conservative intellectual diagnosis assigns blame to what
  many see as a broad presence within the contemporary Western
  Roman Catholic clergy of persons with *homosexual tendencies*.

- By contrast, the progressive intellectual diagnosis, disturbed by
  the conservative blaming of clerics with homosexual tendencies,
  instead puts the blame on *"Clericalism,"* which it sees as a problem-
  atic psychological attitude, or as an authoritarian, non-transparent,
  and unaccountable organizational culture, or as both.

Those two diagnoses fail to get to the root of the problem. The conservative diagnosis fails by engaging in scapegoating, while the progressive diagnosis fails by only addressing Clericalism's surface level.

Even though some scholars have linked (correctly, I believe) the origin
of Western Catholic Clericalism's celibate system to dominance of a
Western medieval homosexual clerical subculture, the conservative diagnosis erroneously and unjustly scapegoats human persons with homosexual tendencies.

It is true that the vast majority of clerical sexual-abuse victims have been boys, and that all the Roman Catholic clerical perpetrators have been adult males.[1] That pattern does indicate a homosexual dimension to the pervasive abuse, but that does not make homosexuality the cause of the abuse. The reason why it does not is that the vast majority of homosexual persons, including clerics with homosexual tendencies, are most certainly not sexual abusers.

An extreme form of the conservative intellectual diagnosis would imply that, if there were no homosexuals in the Roman Catholic clergy, there would be little or no problem with clerical sexual abuse and cover-up in the Roman Catholic Church. But that extreme version of the conservative diagnosis contradicts empirical evidence from the wider society, which documents pervasive sexual abuse of under-age female victims by adult heterosexual males.

Thus, if by waving some magic wand, we could make all the Roman Catholic clergy for the last one-hundred years exclusively heterosexual, while leaving the clerical system as it was (without controls or accountability), evidence from the wider society makes clear that we would expect to find pervasive victimization of girls by a significant minority of such an exclusively heterosexual Roman Catholic Clergy.

The critique of this small book, however, is not primarily directed at the conservative scapegoating. But it is important to state that both homosexual and heterosexual persons are equally made in the Divine image, and that both carry equal beauty and dignity in God's eyes. Further, the Roman Catholic Church has been abundantly blessed by the enormous contributions of both homosexual and heterosexual clerics.

---

[1] Also, within the Roman Catholic clerical-abuse and coverup scandals, it is important to distinguish the narrower but horrendous problem of pedophilia (sexual abuse of pre-pubescent children) from the wider and horrendous sexual abuse of legal minors who are post-pubescent youth, including those in late-teenage years (but still under eighteen years of age). Most cases have been of the latter form.

For that reason, the conservative scapegoating of homosexuals for the current clerical sexual-abuse and coverup scandals, as if homosexuality itself were the cause, blasphemes the image of God in all of us. More narrowly for the purposes of this book, however, *that conservative scapegoating, just like progressive surface-level diagnosis, misses the deeper problem of the systemic nature of Clericalism.*

But it is the so-called "progressive" diagnosis of Clericalism, as the cause of the problem of clerical sexual-abuse and coverup, that this book primarily critiques. Certainly, that progressive diagnosis is correct when it points to serious psychological problems in some clerics, and to serious problems within the clerical organizational culture – for example, authoritarianism, lack of transparency, and unaccountability.

The progressive intellectual diagnosis, however, fails to unveil the deep root of Clericalism as a non-evangelical institution, which inevitably generates problems and even pathologies for each successive clerical generation.

Thus, the progressive intellectual diagnosis is correct to focus on Clericalism, but it fails to an analyze how deeply rooted Clericalism is as an institutional structure within the Roman Catholic Church.

Further, it fails to analyze how the institution of Roman Catholic Clericalism was historically constructed by legislation over more than a millennium and a half, and how that Roman Catholic legislation of Clericalism is now undermining the Western Catholic evangelization.

Deepening that surface-level analysis of Clericalism by the so-called "progressive" intelligentsia of the Western or Roman Catholic Church is the purpose of this small book.

Southwest Florida
September 2018

3

1

INTRODUCTION

CLERICALISM IS AN INSTITUTION

LEGISLATED IN THREE STAGES

S OME MEMBERS OF THE ROMAN CATHOLIC CHURCH think of "Clericalism" as *an arrogant psychological attitude,* found among a minority of Roman Catholic bishops and presbyters ("priests").[1] Others think of it as *an unhealthy organizational culture,* which resists transparency and accountability.

For the minority of Roman Catholic bishops and presbyters who express pathological tendencies through Clericalism, the psychological diagnosis is correct. Certainly too, the organizational culture of Roman Catholic Clericalism is authoritarian and resists transparency and accountability.

---

[1] The New Testament uses the term "presbyter" to refer to the servant-leader office that in later centuries was changed to "priest." That change occurred partly in imitation of the Jewish priesthood, even though Jesus was not a Jewish priest. It also occurred partly in imitation of priests from other religions in the Roman Empire, as the formerly persecuted Christian movement gradually became integrated into the imperial system. In fidelity to the apostolic and New Testament use, this small book prefers the original New Testament name of "presbyter," rather than the later non-evangelical change of the name to "priest."

But the root of Roman Catholic Clericalism is neither a psychological attitude nor an organizational culture. Rather, and at a far deeper level, *Clericalism is an institution historically constructed by legislation.*

Further, Clericalism was not part of Jesus' humbling and egalitarian vision for his community of disciples. He harshly rejected the attitude, culture, and institution of what we today call "Clericalism." Indeed, Jesus declared:

> *You know how those who exercise authority among the Gentiles lord it over them; their great ones make their importance felt. It cannot be that way with you. Anyone among you who aspires to greatness must serve the rest, and whoever wants to rank first among you, must serve the needs of all.* (Matthew 20:25-26)

Jesus also declared:

> *The Scribes and the Pharisees have succeeded Moses as teachers; therefore, do everything they tell you. But do not follow their example. Their words are bold, but their deeds are few.*
>
> *They bind up heavy loads, hard to carry, to lay on others' shoulders, while they themselves will not lift a finger to budge them. They widen their phylacteries and wear huge tassels. They are fond of places of honor at banquets and the front seats at synagogues, of marks of respect in public places, and being called 'Rabbi.'* [2]
>
> *As to you, avoid the title 'Rabbi.' One among you is your teacher, the rest are learners. Do not call any-one on earth your father. Only one is your father, the One in heaven. Avoid being called teachers. Only one is your teacher, the Messiah.*
>
> *The greatest among you will be the one who serves the rest. Whoever exalts himself shall be humbled, but whoever humbles himself shall be exalted.* (Matthew 23:1-12)

---

[2] The Hebrew title "Rabbi" literally means "my master," with "master" signifying master of the Torah and implying master teacher of the Torah.

Clericalism as an
Historically Legislated Institution

Clericalism, which the Roman Catholic Church's Canon Law juridically calls the "Clerical State" (meaning "clerical class"), had its ancient foundation in imperial legislation. In the late-classical era, the Roman Empire through law 'elevated' ordained Christian leaders to the privileged and protected imperial class ("state") called "clergy."

That legal construction of Christian "clergy," as a privileged and protected imperial class, did not occur until the 4th Century, that is, not until approximately 300 years after the Pentecostal birth of the Christian movement. Prior to that point, such imperial rights and protection had been given only to priests of imperially recognized pagan religions, and not to the servant-leaders of Jesus' community of disciples, who had earlier been persecuted by the imperial state.

The 4th-Century historical construction of Clericalism – again, granting special legal rights and protections to Christian "clergy" – took the form of imperial legislation. That legislation was issued during the historical period when the Empire was being Christianized, initially by the Emperor Constantine the Great (ruling from 306 to 337) and more fully by his successors.[3]

Clearly then, Clericalism is not of apostolic origin, and so it is also not evangelical. Rather, Clericalism was *historically constructed as an institution through late-classical imperial legislation*. As such, Clericalism constitutes a juridical-sociological institution imposed upon, but distinct from, the evangelical servant-leadership offices of episcopate, presbyterate, and deaconate.

---

[3] That extensive imperial legislation on "clergy" and related matters was subsequently gathered into Book I, Title III, of the CODEX THEODOSIANUS, a collection of imperial decrees since the year 312.AD that was officially promulgated in the Eastern Empire in 438 AD and in the Western Empire in 439 AD. See: *https://droitromain.univ-grenoble-alpes.fr/Codex_Theod.htm.*

Again, beginning with what I call the "Constantinian-imperial inversion" (which will be addressed in Chapter 3), Clericalism was initially founded as an imperially legislated institution. In that context, it had *a functional role* (albeit a non-evangelical one), namely, to serve as an important functioning part of the church-state partnership established by the Constantinian Empire.

Further, as we will see in later chapters of this book, the Clerical State's functional (but again non-evangelical) role was later expanded for the Western or Roman Catholic Church through two subsequent developments:

- First, during the 11th and 12th Centuries, through the Gregorian popes' legislation of *Clerical Celibacy*, as a foundational part of the theocratic church-state integration for the papacy's new "temporal power" within high-medieval Christendom;

- Second, during the 16th Century, through the Council of Trent's legislation of the *Clerical Seminary* as a foundational part of the new and modern Western Catholic Counter-Reformation, which lasted for four hundred years until the Second Ecumenical Council of the Vatican (during the second half of the 20th Century).

"Clergy" as a Misapplied Name for Ordained Servant-Leaders in the Christian Community

The word "clergy," for which "clerical" is the adjective, comes from the New Testament's use of the Greek word "*kleros*." That Greek word means "inheritance" or "lot," but it also came to mean "chosen," as in chosen for inheritance or chosen by lot.

In the New Testament, scholars point to the use of *kleros* in 1 Peter 5:3 (in the accusative case *kleron*) as referring to the "chosen" People of God, just as Israel is a "chosen people." Thus, the *kleros,* which is translated into English as "clergy," signifies not the ordained leaders of the Christian community, but rather the "chosen" Christian community, which is also called in Greek the holy and priestly *Laos* (from which we get the English word "laity").

Verse 1 of the Greek text for 1 Peter 5 is addressed to "presbyters" (*presbyteroi*), which the New American Bible translates as "elders." That name clearly refers to pastors. since the presbyters are urged in verse 2 to "shepherd" (*poimanate*) "God's flock" (*poimnion tou Theou*),

Then, in verse 3, the presbyters are told not to "lord-over" (in Greek *katakyrieuontes*) the *kleron* (again, meaning the "chosen" *Laos* as the People of God).[4] Yet the New American Bible translation obscures the meaning of *kleron* by mistranslating it as "those assigned to you." The late classical Latin translation, however, remained faithful to the Greek original by translating *kleron* as "*cleris*." That translation tells the presbyters as shepherds not to "lord-over" the "clergy" (*neque ut dominantes in cleris*) – again, with "clergy"(*cleris*) meaning the "chosen" People of God).

Thus, a strictly literal translation, following both the original Greek version and the late-classical Latin version, would be read as directing the presbyters (elders) not to lord-over the "chosen" (*kleron* in Greek, "*cleris*" in Latin, and "clergy" in English). To repeat yet again: in 1 Peter 5:3, *kleron* refers to the community of Jesus' disciples (the People of God) as the "chosen," for whom the presbyters serve as shepherds.

For that reason, the later use of "clergy." as referring instead to the ordained servant-leaders of Jesus' "chosen" community of disciples,

---

[4] In the high-medieval period, Roman Catholic bishops, as part of the medieval church-state theocracy, were given the title "lord" – a title which contradicts the very "lording over" forbidden by 1 Peter 5:3. Still today, "higher clergy" at various organizational levels are given anti-evangelical "lording-over" titles like "monsignor" (originally meaning "my lord"), "your excellency," "your grace," "your eminence," and "your holiness." And still today, "higher clergy" wear exotic and costly ceremonial costumes, with aristocratic origins, that visually signify aristocratic "lording-over." Of course, neither Jesus nor his apostles used lordly titles or wore lordly costumes.

represents *an upside-down ecclesiology*. It wrongly portrays only the ordained servant-leaders as the "chosen" ones.

Further, contemporary church language refers to the ordained as "having a vocation." But that repeated misuse of *kleron* ("clergy") obscures the New Testament's teaching that the "chosen" Christian community has the fundamental "vocation."

Transition from a Functional to a Dysfunctional, & Sometimes Pathological Institution

Today, most of Western Civilization has rejected the past Roman Catholic church-state integration, within which Clericalism formerly played a functional role. That functionality was the case not only for the Constantinian Empire, but also both for medieval Roman Catholic Christendom and for the modern Roman Catholic Counter-Reformation, as well as for modern Lutheran and Calvinist forms of a Protestant church-state alliance.

In the case of the United States, where from its beginning there was no established religion, there nonetheless existed a non-legislated but still functioning church-state partnership culturally presided over by the Protestant establishment. Until the second half of the 20th Century, that culturally rooted Protestant church-state alliance functioned through the practices (if not legislation) of government, education, and other Protestant-dominated institutions.

Further, in the post-World War II period, Catholic "clergy" began to be partially included within that cultural partnership.

But, with the postmodern Electronic Revolution during the second half of the 20th Century, and particularly through postmodern electronic communications media, capitalist business corporations increasingly took command of Western public culture, and especially through advertising and entertainment.

That development has now produced a Western corporate-capitalist cultural hegemony. Further, that new corporate cultural hegemony promotes *the late-modern Western ideology of Secular Materialism*, which celebrates "individualism," "pleasure," and "success" (all measured only by money) as dominant cultural values for the socialization of youth.

Thus, Western Roman Catholic Clericalism now exists within the expanding public cultural framework of Western Secular Materialism. Within that late-modern cultural framework, Roman Catholic Clericalism has inevitably become *dysfunctional*.

Again, the reason is that the institution of Clericalism was legally designed for a public functional role within church-state partnerships (again, first late-classical, then high-medieval, and finally modern). But such church-state partnerships no longer exist within the cultural context of late-modern Western Secular Materialism.

Therefore, because there is no longer a church-state partnership in most of Western Civilization, and because contemporary Western public culture promotes Secular Materialism, Western Roman Catholic Clericalism has now become a marginal and even eccentric institution lacking any public function.

Stripped of its historical function within a church-state partnership, and increasingly loosing public cultural legitimation, Roman Catholic Clericalism is now grounded only in church legislation.

To repeat: the late-modern historical form of Roman Catholic Clericalism has now mutated into a sociological institution that has become not only dysfunctional but also marginal and eccentric.

Roman Catholic Clericalism does, however, retain a publicly colorful and theatrical ceremonial legacy from its monarchical and aristocratic past (e.g., scarlet robes for cardinals, gold and jeweled vestments, as well as gold and silver chalices for liturgies, etc.).

But, in a manner similar to the British monarchy, Roman Catholic Clericalism's public impact, apart from its public scandals, has now become largely limited to theatrical spectacles. Yet, Roman Catholic clerical theatrical spectacles are overwhelmingly male, while the British monarch has had female queens. For both, however, the public (including the Catholic laity in the church case) mainly plays the role of spectator.

Further, despite its male-theatrical power, the Roman Catholic clerical performance-model of spectacle-and-spectator does not spiritually empower a lay-centered evangelization. Indeed, it works against lay empowerment, both culturally and spiritually.

In addition, although the diminishment of the Roman Catholic institution of Clericalism to a marginal and eccentric phenomenon may appear harmless, in fact it is not.

Rather, certain pathological tendencies within the institution of Roman Catholic Clericalism (e.g., sexual and financial abuses and coverups), which were long kept out of public view by its political power, have now become exposed to public scrutiny by the media. That in turn has precipitated extensive public outrage.

Further, many observers judge that the now dysfunctional institution of Roman Catholic Clericalism for some time has attracted a significant number of marginal and eccentric candidates, as well as a minority of pathological candidates who have caused seemingly endless public scandals.

Mostly significantly, the late-modern dysfunctional and scandalous public image of Roman Catholic Clericalism undermines Catholic evangelization in the West by blocking the evangelizing power of the laity in two ways.

- First, because of its eccentric and marginal role, late-modern Roman Catholic Clericalism grows pastorally distant from, and often out of touch with, the everyday lives of ordinary Catholic families and individuals, and especially with the lives of contemporary youth.

- Second, because its public scandals of sexual (and financial) abuse and coverup provoke public disgust, late-modern Roman Catholic Clericalism has become *anti-evangelical,* that is, it drives people away from the Roman Catholic Church.

The late-modern dysfunctional form of Roman Catholic Clericalism now impedes evangelization even by the many devoted and even saintly Western Catholic bishops and presbyters. For they cannot escape their late-modern sociological identity as institutionally privileged members of the now dysfunctional, marginalized, eccentric, and sometimes pathological institution of Western Roman Catholic Clericalism.

Need to Canonically Dismantle the Historically Constructed Institution of Roman Catholic Clericalism

It should be now clear that, to resolve these problems and to renew Catholic evangelization within Western Civilization (and to strengthen its postcolonial global flourishing), Roman Catholic Clericalism now needs to be gradually and prudentially dismantled.

Again, because the Roman Catholic institution of Clericalism was historically constructed through imperial, papal, and conciliar legislation, because the public political functions for which it was legislated no longer exist, because its internal pathologies have become scandalous, and because it was not part of Jesus' evangelical vision, it now can and should be historically dismantled within the Canon Law and ministerial structures of the Roman Catholic Church.

Further, Roman Catholic Clericalism now needs to be dismantled in order to liberate *an authentically postmodern[5] proclamation of Jesus'*

---

[5] As explained in many of my earlier writings, many phenomena that are described by many intellectuals as "postmodern" are not authentically so. Rather, they are only *late-*

13

Gospel. Such postmodern canonical dismantling, however, will be a complex process requiring the gradualist and prudent exercise of practical wisdom.

Further, that canonical dismantling will require *an authentically postmodern spiritual, intellectual, and juridical Catholic renaissance*. It will also presumably require *an authentically postmodern ecumenical council*. Further, that council will need to bring together as evangelical equals *all twenty-four Catholic Churches*, which constitute what I call the "Global Catholic Communion."

The Roman Catholic Church as Only
One Church within the Global Catholic Communion

In addressing the institutional problem of Roman Catholic Clericalism, we need to remember that the Roman Catholic Church is but one Catholic Church within the Global Catholic Communion. Together, the twenty-four Catholic Churches within the Global Catholic Communion constitute the fullness of what may be called the "Global Catholic Church."

Twenty-three of these Catholic Churches – all historically distinct from the Western, Latin, or Roman Catholic Church – are named the "Eastern Catholic Churches." In a prejudice of diminishment, however, voices in the Western Church often speak of these Eastern Churches as only "rites." But they are in fact *sui juris* Catholic Churches, equal in ecclesiological stature (though not in political power) to the Roman Catholic Church. Further, their roots are found not in Rome or the West, but in Africa, Arabia, Eastern Europe, and India.

---

modern, as well as dysfunctional and sometimes pathologically so. For more on what is authentically postmodern, see my earlier book POSTMODERN ECOLOGICAL SPIRITUALITY: *Catholic-Christian Hope for the Dawn of a Postmodern Ecological Civilization Arising from within the Spiritual Dark Night of Modern Industrial Civilization* (Pacem in Terris Press, 2017).

Of course, the Roman Catholic Church is the giant among the twenty-four Catholic Churches comprising the Global Catholic Communion. That is because, since the time of Charlemagne and more so since the so-called 'Gregorian Reform' of the high-medieval period, and even more so since the modern European mercantile invasion of the Americas and subsequent modern industrial colonialism, leaders of the Roman Catholic Church developed what I have called sociologically the "Imperial Church" of Western Christian Civilization.

Until recently, and for approximately one thousand and seven-hundred years, the Roman Catholic Church functioned as the religious partner in violent forms of Western 'Christian' imperial colonialism and neocolonialism. Because of that religious partnership, the Roman Catholic Church received vast territorial 'prizes' from Western imperial colonialism. But, of course, the cultural identities of the colonized peoples within those territories were hardly "Roman."

But the "Eastern Churches" did not participate in Western imperialism and colonialism, and so they are free of that negative legacy. Further, many of the twenty-three non-Roman Catholic Churches go back to the very beginning of Christianity, and they often carry evangelical gifts that have been diminished in the Western Church. In addition, practically all these Eastern churches still reject the Western or Roman Catholic non-evangelical innovation of mandatory Clerical Celibacy for diocesan presbyters.

For all these reasons, I believe that the Eastern Catholic Churches – if freed from restraints often imposed upon them by Roman "ecclesiastical imperialism" – will show, and indeed are already beginning to show, charismatic potential for an authentically postmodern global "New Evangelization."

Yet historically, global evangelization by the Eastern Catholic Churches tended to be blocked by the Western or Roman Catholic Church. By implicitly acting as if Jesus' missionary mandate to preach the Gospel to the whole world belonged *only* to the Western or Roman Catholic Church, leaders of the Western "Imperial Church" implicitly denied that the Eastern Catholic Churches, as part of the Global Catholic Communion, also carry that same universal missionary mandate.

In that "ecclesiastical imperialism," Western or Roman Catholic leaders often attempted to limit the missionary mandate of the Eastern Catholic Churches to specific ethnic populations and to specific ethnic territories. Thus, in practice if not in theory, they heretically denied that Jesus gave to all twenty-four Catholic Churches the universal mission to preach the Gospel of Jesus to the entire world.

Let us now examine a brief historical overview of the legislated construction of Clericalism as a non-evangelical institution. This overview will summarize how Catholic Clericalism was constructed in three stages, one legislated for both the Eastern and Western Churches, and the other two legislated only for the Western or Roman Catholic Church. (Subsequent chapters in this book will examine these three historical stages of legislation in greater detail.)

Three Historical Stages in
the Non-Evangelical Legislation of Clericalism

Again, Catholic Clericalism is a non-evangelical institution that was constructed by legislation in three historical stages. We may describe those three historical stages, which span more than a millennium and a half, as: 1) Constantinian Clerical State; 2) Gregorian Clerical Celibacy; and 3) Tridentine Clerical Seminary.

STAGE 1 - CONSTANTINIAN CLERICAL STATE
Late-Classical Legislation of the
Imperial Clerical Class

During the late-classical 4th Century, when the Roman Empire became Christian, the special "state" (again, imperial class) for "clergy,"

16

formerly assigned by imperial legislation to pagan priests, was transferred by imperial legislation to Christian bishops and presbyters.

Through this first cultural-historical form of Clericalism as a legal class, the New Testament's servant-leadership model for bishops and presbyters was inverted into an imperial-clerical *lording-over* the Christian *Laos* (laity).

As we have seen, Chapter 5 Verse 3 of the New Testament's First Epistle of Peter explicitly forbids that church leaders "*lord-over*" (*katakyri-euontes*) Jesus' "*chosen*" (*kleron*), meaning the chosen *Laos*. "Lording-over," it states, is the way of "the gentiles" (at that time meaning the Roman Empire).

Again, according to 1 Peter 5:3, "lording-over" is forbidden to the Christian movement's ordained servant-leaders. Yet, with the 4th-Century Constantinian inversion, Catholic bishops and presbyters became redefined as "lording-over" religious agents of the Roman Empire.

By historically constructing the Clerical State as an imperial class for ordained bishops and presbyters in both the Eastern and the Western Churches, that imperial legislation sociologically reshaped Catholic Christianity into the Imperial Church of the now Christianized Roman Empire.

STAGE 2 - GREGORIAN CLERICAL CELIBACY
High-Medieval Papal Legislation of the Clerical State
as a Monastic-like Celibate Caste

Centuries later, with the high-medieval consolidation of papal "temporal power," a new alliance of church and state emerged in the West for the Holy Roman Empire of "Christendom." The papal "temporal power" had begun earlier during the 7th-Century under Charlemagne.

Then, in the "High Middle Ages," it expanded theocratically with the so-called 'Gregorian Reform.'[6]

During the 11th and 12th Centuries, the 'Gregorian Reform' cruelly imposed its new papal legislation demanding *Clerical Celibacy* on Western Catholic bishops and presbyters. That 'Reform' had to be imposed by police force, since at the time most Western Catholic diocesan bishops and presbyters were married, as had been the case for most diocesan bishops and presbyters in a long tradition that reaches back to apostolic times and is grounded in the New Testament.

Inspired both by papal lust for theocratic power and by misogynist spiritual corruptions within major sectors of Benedictine monasticism, the 'Gregorian Reform' showed no concern for the wives and children of those traditionally married Western Catholic bishops and presbyters. Some were even forced into slavery, including for the papal Lateran Palace.

By sociologically uprooting Western Catholic bishops and presbyters from the wider Catholic kinship system, and by converting them into a monastic-like celibate caste, that high-medieval papal legislation attempted to produce celibate-clerical cadres who would be loyal to expanding papal theocratic power within the high-medieval feudal system of the Holy Roman Empire.

---

[6] The Catholic papacy's "temporal power" refers to the popes' past function as political kings over papally controlled regions (the "Papal States") in what is today's Italy. While the "temporal power" goes back to the early medieval period, the independence of the Papal States only officially began in the 12th Century, when the Treaty of Venice recognized the independence of the vast Papal States from the Holy Roman Empire. Throughout the 18th and 19th Centuries, however, the popes began to lose control of their territories. Finally, in 1870, when Italian troops captured Rome during the Franco-Prussian War, the Papal States ceased to exist. After that, the popes became "prisoners of the Vatican," which had become Italian territory. Later, with the 1927 Lateran Treaty negotiated between the Holy See and the Italian fascist dictator Benito Mussolini, the small territory of the Vatican became an independent city-state, called in Italian *Stato della Città del Vaticano*.

STAGE 3 - TRIDENTINE CLERICAL SEMINARY
Early-Modern Conciliar Legislation of
Monastic-Like Clerical Educational Institutions

Much later, during the early-modern 16th Century, the new spiritual and social consciousness of the rising bourgeois class (still enmeshed within aristocratic societies) began to spread across Western and Central Europe through the Protestant Reformation, and especially via the printer's guild in Northern-European university towns.

In strategic defense, the still aristocratic Western episcopacy of the Catholic Counter-Reformation mandated, though the Council of Trent, the educational segregation of candidates for ordination in a monastic-like Clerical Seminary.

Intellectually segregating clerical "seminarians" from Catholic universities, and spiritually segregating them from Catholic lay professors and students (especially from women), the Tridentine seminary system attempted to 'protect' Roman Catholic candidates for ordination from early-modern bourgeois-Protestant influences, and to counter the high incidence of Roman Catholic presbyters living in common-law marriages (referred to by the Council of Trent as "concubinage").

The Roman Catholic Tridentine seminary thus became a key strategic element for the Roman Catholic Counter-Reformation's resistance to the Protestant acceptance of "clerical marriage," and to the Protestant emphasis on the evangelical vocation of the laity.

Contemporary Breakdown of Clericalism across
its Three-Part Institutional Structure

Taken all together, those three historical but non-evangelical stages of legislation – again, first imperial, then papal, and finally conciliar – still survive in the modern canonical Roman Catholic Clerical State, which is still overlaid on diocesan bishops and presbyters within the Roman

Catholic Church. That overlay constitutes the modern male "*clerical-celibate-seminary*" institution of Roman Catholic Clericalism.[7]

Yet, as pointed out earlier, that three-part male "clerical-celibate-seminary" institution of modern Roman Catholic Clericalism is now breaking down. In the late-modern secular-materialist context of Western Civilization, the historically constructed institution of Clericalism has become sociologically dysfunctional, as well as culturally marginal and eccentric, and sometimes pathologically criminal. *As a result, the Western Catholic evangelization is also breaking down.*

Yet, despite the breakdown of Roman Catholic Clericalism, we find hope in the creative spiritual response that the Holy Spirit is inspiring through *an authentically postmodern "New Evangelization."* That New Evangelization, while still only seminal, is emerging in non-clerical lay form, and especially through feminine, postcolonial, and indigenous energies of spiritual regeneration. Also, this New Evangelization is developing primarily within the Global South, while major sectors of European and European-American populations of the Roman Catholic Church remain trapped within the collapsing "Old Evangelization" (still dependent on Clericalism), and within the wider cultural-spiritual crisis of late-modern Western Civilization.

But some emerging forms of this new lay spiritual energy also remain imprisoned within the late-modern bourgeois conscious, which is hyper-masculine and still carries the modern Western imperial-colonial legacy. By contrast, authentically postmodern and truly post-bourgeois forms of regenerative lay energy need to be grounded in what I have called "Postmodern Ecological Spirituality." Exploring that

---

[7] In the Roman Catholic Church, the Clerical State also applies to ordained "permanent" deacons, but with two variants. First, they may be married (but only once) and, second, they are 'exempt' for the canonical guarantee of economic support, which is required by canonical legislation for bishops and presbyters. Further, as already noted, "seminarians" in "major seminaries" were until 1972 admitted to the Clerical State.

regenerative spirituality, however, and exploring the regenerative lay energies bringing it forth, is beyond the scope of this book.

Again, my earlier-mentioned book, titled POSTMODERN ECOLOGICAL SPIRITUALITY, has attempted an initial exploration of those emerging spiritual energies of regeneration. After publishing that book, I further explored one of its themes in my also already-noted small book. THE CRUEL ELEVENTH-CENTURY IMPOSITION OF CLERICAL CELIBACY. Now, in this new book titled ROMAN CATHOLIC CLERICALISM, I offer a deeper and broader exploration of the wider theme of Clericalism.[8]

In the next chapter of this book, we will recall how Jesus opposed Clericalism and how the "Way" of Jesus remains lay. Then, in successive chapters, we will explore in greater detail the three historical stages for the legislation of Catholic Clericalism – again, first imperial, then papal, and finally conciliar. Lastly, in the book's Conclusion, we will explore the question: "What is to be done?"

In addition, the book includes in its Appendix a short essay, originally published in Commonweal Magazine, that distinguishes the Clerical State from the Sacrament of Orders. That essay argues that the former needs to be eliminated, while the latter needs to be preserved.

---

[8] Relevant sections from those two earlier books have been inserted in this new book and adapted to its exploration of Clericalism.

2

THE "WAY" OF JESUS IS LAY

THE CLERICAL-LAY DISTINCTION
IS NOT EVANGELICAL

I N ORDER TO UNDERSTAND THE DEEP SPIRITUAL REASONS for the late-modern institutional breakdown of the clericalized form of the Western Catholic episcopate and presbyterate, we need first to remember the foundational "lay" nature of the original messianic movement that Jesus founded. Today, we call that movement "church," but its originally Hebrew and Greek names are better translated as "gathering" or "community," and they signify a *lay* gathering or community.

In Jesus' original "gathering," and in the early church, there was no clerical-lay distinction or division. The "Way"[1] of Jesus was (and still is) only *lay*. The institution of Clericalism was never part of Jesus' "Way," and so it is not evangelical. For that reason, this chapter addresses the non-clerical and lay nature of the "Way" of Jesus, both during his life and in early Christianity.

---

[1] In the New Testament and in the early Church, the Christian movement was often called the "Way." That name meant following the way or path of Jesus.

Jesus as a Lay Person

In the four Gospels, Jesus is never portrayed as a Jewish priest. He is rather portrayed as a Galilean lay person and a rabbi, which in the Judaism of his time was a lay teaching office. Indeed, Jesus deliberately did not engage with the Temple priests in Jerusalem, but he was willing to dialogue, even if polemically, with the lay "Scribes and Pharisees."[2]

Of course, Jesus was also never a member of the "clergy," since the Clerical State was not constructed for Christianity until the early 4th Century. Still today, for Catholic Christianity, the Clerical State needs to be clearly understood by the entire Church as distinct from the Sacrament of Orders.

The one and only place in the entire New Testament where Jesus is called "priest," and in fact "high-priest," is in the Epistle to the Hebrews, which according to scholars is not a letter but rather a treatise and may have been written late in the 2nd Century. Yet even Hebrews states that Jesus was not a Jewish priest, but rather one according to the "order of Melchizedek, King of Salem." Thus, the author of Hebrews wrote: " It is clear that our Lord arose from Judah, and in regard to that tribe Moses said nothing about priests" (Chapter 7, Verse 14).

Apart from that one exceptional statement in Hebrews, the New Testament never refers to Jesus, or to the early bishops (*episcopoi*) or presbyters (*presbyteroi*) as "priests." Rather, a literal translation of those titles is simply "supervisors" and "elders," though clearly those offices carried the authority of servant-leadership within the community of Jesus' disciples.

Also, we need to recall that the four Gospels portray Jesus as gathering an egalitarian movement, and even an upside-down version of

---

[2] On Jesus' lay identity and his now engaging in dialogue with the Temple priesthood, see John P. Meier, A MARGINAL JEW: *Rethinking the Historical Jesus, Volume One: The Roots of the Problem and the Person* (Doubleday, 1991), pp. 345-249

"hierarchy" – a community in which all are brothers and sisters united in love, in which the last shall be first, and in which the leaders are to function as humble servants.

Of course, for the Catholic tradition, it is theologically legitimate to speak of Jesus as "priest" and "high priest," just as it is legitimate to speak of the priestly nature of the Sacrament of Orders, as well as the "priesthood" of the entire community of Jesus' disciples – even while theologically distinguishing their different meanings.

But such is not the typical language of the New Testament, nor of the early community of Jesus' disciples. Nor is it helpful in empowering laity for the postmodern New Evangelization.

Pre-Imperial Christianity
as an Evangelical Lay Movement

The brutal Roman Empire crucified Jesus as a Jewish lay teacher (rabbi) and prophet, because the imperial authority perceived him as a political threat to the Empire.

The Empire also subsequently executed Peter and Paul, both Jewish laypersons, as well as thousands of other early Christians, all of whom were lay. That foundational Christian period has been called the "Age of Martyrs," since the Empire executed so many Christians for following the "Way" of Jesus, which is lay.

Throughout the Apostolic Era and into the Age of Martyrs, Christians following the "Way" of Jesus remained exclusively lay. As we have seen, in those foundational eras of pre-Imperial Christianity, there was for Christianity no such thing as the "Clerical State." It was a later legal construction for Catholic Christianity.

Again, early on, there had emerged disciples of Jesus who were ordained for authority-bearing offices, namely deacons, presbyters, and bishops, as well as disciples of Jesus with special charisms for the wider community of disciples, including communities of virgins and widows. Yet all were lay.

And again, in those early centuries of the Christian movement, there was originally only the one path, which was not "clerical." It was the one lay "Way" of Jesus' baptized disciples, including ordained lay leaders and lay disciples with special charisms. To repeat: there was only the one "Way" of Jesus' own lay path.

Holy & Chosen People of God

The word "lay" comes from the Greek word *laos*, which means "people." In the Greek Septuagint translation of the Hebrew Scriptures and in Greek texts of the New Testament, *laos* means the holy, royal, and priestly People of God. Further, as we have seen, in the New Testament the Greek work *kleros* (again, from which the word "clergy" is derived) means "chosen." And the New Testament uses the word *kleros* to signify that the *Laos* of Jesus' disciples is "chosen."

For that reason, and again as we have seen, the canonical Clerical State is not a constitutive dimension of the Catholic Church. It did not exist in the foundational early centuries of Christianity, and its very name is based on *a misinterpretation* of the New Testament's use of the Greek word *kleros* (the chosen).

Further, the canonical Clerical State is not a sacrament. Even so, in the Western Catholic Church at least, it often became elevated in practice above the "laity," and thus above the sacraments of Baptism, Confirmation, and Marriage.

In summary, the Clerical State represented a non-evangelical compromise that integrated Catholic Christianity within the Roman Empire. That compromise later carried over into medieval and modern forms of church-state integration within different societal systems. But, again, Clericalism was not part of the "Way" of Jesus' lay path, and its introduction weakened the understanding of Jesus' Gospel message.

And now, without an official church-state partnership, the Clerical State has become dysfunctional, as well as marginal and eccentric, and sometimes pathological.

In the next three chapters, we review the three historical stages in the legislative construction of the non-evangelical institution of Clericalism. We begin with the Clerical State.

3

STAGE 1 - CLERICAL STATE

LATE-CLASSICAL LEGISLATION BY

THE CONSTANTINIAN EMPIRE

I N THE EARLY 4ᵀᴴ Century of the first Christian millennium, Roman imperial leaders saw the lay movement of Christianity   al
ready spread throughout the Empire – as offering the possibility of
holding together the externally threatened and internally disintegrat-
ing imperial society.

As external attacks by migrating 'barbarian' Germanic tribes intensified, and as the Empire began to degenerate internally, the lay Christian movement appeared to imperial leaders to offer unifying organizational strength. That was because the unifying Christian cosmopoli-
tan vision was not limited to any specific geographic, ethnic, or class
identity.

End of Persecuted Lay Church
& Rise of Imperial-Hierarchical Church

From the time of the 57th Roman Emperor, Constantine the Great (272-
337) who ruled from Constantinople (formerly Byzantium and now Is-
tanbul in today's Turkey), the imperial government constructed an ec-
clesial-political alliance with the bishops of the imperial regions (then
called "dioceses").

The Roman Empire, which had crucified Jesus and probably thousands of his followers, appealed to the episcopal leaders of Jesus' disciples in the desperate hope of saving itself. Most bishops accepted the invitation, though the Coptic Church of Africa resisted imperial domination and later suffered persecution from the Imperial State in its new partnership with what I have sociologically called the "Imperial Church."

In sum, Catholic Christianity became the official religion of the Empire, reshaped by imperial consciousness and restructuring, and backed by the coercive power of the Imperial State.

Within that profound ecclesial-societal shift, the first history of the Catholic Church, written by the Eastern Catholic bishop Eusebius of Caesarea (c. 263-339), who was close to the imperial household, described the Emperor Constantine ruling on his throne as reflecting an imperial image of God.[1]

To strengthen that fourth-century episcopal-imperial alliance, the Emperor Constantine gave to the Catholic bishops in many towns an imperial building for their gatherings. The Greek word for emperor is *basileus*, so those imperial buildings were called (in English translation) "basilicas," meaning buildings of the Emperor. Imperial basilicas thus became the first large church buildings.

Prior to that gift of imperial buildings, the community of Jesus' disciples had typically gathered during three centuries for the Lord's Supper in people's homes, and often in the large homes of wealthy women. Following the donation of imperial buildings to the Catholic bishops, however, a tendency emerged to reconceptualize the "Church" as *holy buildings*, rather than as the holy community of Jesus' chosen and priestly *Laos*. Still today, we speak of "going to church."

---

[1] See EUSEBIUS: THE CHURCH HISTORY, transl. Paul L. Maier (Kraeger, 2007).

Non-Evangelical Nature
of the Imperial "Clerical State"

Again, with the new alliance between the Catholic bishops and the Roman Empire, imperial leaders also gave to the bishops and to their presbyters the special class-rank held beforehand by the imperially approved pagan priests. That special imperial class-rank is the legal origin of the Clerical State (again, with "state" meaning social class).

That imperial class legally gave to Jesus' ordained disciples certain government-granted economic and political privileges that Jesus' non-ordained disciples did not receive – for example, exemption from imperial taxes and from military service in the imperial army, plus a legal court only for those in the Clerical State.

Yet the Clerical State and the Sacrament of Ordination are distinct. Their distinction is clear from the fact that the Western or Roman Catholic canonical requirement of Clerical Celibacy for diocesan presbyters is linked not theologically to ordination but juridically to the Clerical State.

For that reason, a contemporary ordained clerical-celibate presbyter in the Roman Catholic Church may be released from the obligation of Clerical Celibacy by "reduction (*sic*) to the lay state" – in the Latin rescripts, "*reducionem ad statum laicalem.*"[2]

Yet after that "reduction" or "laicization," the individual remains theologically an ordained presbyter. But, by Canon Law, he is no longer a member of the Clerical State. And, as a "lay person" (despite being in the same ecclesial "state" as Jesus and the apostles), he is canonically

---

[2] Of course, in the Emperor Constantine's late-classical period, there was no mandatory requirement of Clerical Celibacy" in either the Western or the Eastern Churches. That requirement would not come until the 'high' Medieval period, and then only for the Western Church. Further, at the Ecumenical Council of Nicaea, convened in 325 by Constantine, the Catholic bishops, gathered at the Council, explicitly rejected the anti-apostolic proposal from fanatical zealots to impose celibacy on diocesan "clergy."

forbidden to function as a presbyter – again, despite his still valid ordination.

Once again, as we have seen, the Greek word *kleros*, from which the word "clergy" is derived, refers in the Greek texts of the New Testament to the "chosen" character of all disciples of Jesus who form the holy *Laos* (1 Peter 2:5-10). Yet, with the Constantinian imperial-episcopal alliance, the New Testament's lay term *kleros* became misidentified with a 'higher' clerical class non-evangelically "lording over" the non-clerical members of Jesus' holy and priestly *Laos*.

As a result, in addition to the non-evangelical tendency to identify "church" with *temple-like buildings*, a non-evangelical tendency also emerged to identify *clericalized bishops and presbyters* as "the Church," rather than the full *Laos* of all Jesus' disciples.[3]

In addition, that Constantinian episcopal-imperial alliance geographically expanded the Christian evangelization of Western Civilization. It often did so, however, through military force imposed on so-called 'uncivilized' (meaning not living in cities) European tribal peoples.

Much later, during the second millennium of Christianity, that same violent process would be inflicted on so-called 'uncivilized' non-European tribal peoples, who were conquered first by European mercantile colonialism and later by European and European-American industrial colonialism and neo-colonialism.

---

[3] Still today, many people (including many journalists) speak or write about "the church," when they are in fact describing the bishops or the bishops and presbyters (the clerical class). In logic, that error is called the "fallacy of composition," which mistakenly ascribes the whole to what is only a part.

Three Anti-Evangelical Distortions
of Imperial Clericalization

Along with its contributions, that late classical Constantinian episco-pal-imperial alliance created three anti-evangelical distortions within the originally only lay community of Jesus' disciples.

- *Diminishment of Laity.* First, it weakened consciousness of the foundational evangelical truth that the Church is the "lay" (again, from the Greek word *laos*) and "chosen" (again, from the Greek word from *kleros*) community of Jesus' disciples. As we have seen, it did that by precipitating a wrong understanding that the Church is an institution identified with set of temple-like buildings and with a hierarchical-clerical class that received imperial privileges which the rest of Jesus' disciples did not receive.

- *Hierarchical-Clerical Class.* Second, it weakened the foundational evangelical command that the ordained leaders of Jesus' disciples were to function as servant-leaders of the wider lay community. It did that by the social construction, through imperial legislation, of an imperially privileged clerical class empowered by the Imperial State hierarchically to "lord-over" over the "laity" (the holy and chosen *Laos*). Of course, the word "hierarchy," still so commonly used for Western Catholic bishops, does not appear anywhere in the New Testament.

As the imperially clericalized bishops became integrated with the militaristic imperial State, many bishops adopted the hierarchical "lording-over" style of exercising authority over the "lay" members of the Catholic community. Yet that hierarchical-patriarchal and military-command style of authority constituted the very anti-evangelical "lording-over" (*katakyrieuontes*) forbidden in 1 Peter 5:3.

- *Cross as Imperial Military Conquest.* Third, the late-classical Constantinian imperial-episcopal alliance undermined the foundational evangelical doctrine of the Cross as a symbol of persecution. That undermining not only legitimated imperial, class-based, and gender-based domination. It also inverted the meaning of the Cross – from Jesus' non-violent suffering of execution by the Empire to clerical support for the Empire's violent conquest of tribal peoples.

As a symbol of that third distortion of Christianity, we have the legend of Constantine seeing in a vision the Cross of the non-violent Jesus, with Greek words that have been traditionally rendered in Latin as "*In hoc signo vinces*" (under this sign you will conquer). Thus, the prophetic meaning of the Cross of Jesus was turned upside down. No longer a symbol of imperial persecution, the Cross became disfigured as a symbol of military conquest, and in the name of an imperial Christian Civilization.[4]

Again, that social-sin of linking evangelization with imperial violence continued for Western Catholic Christianity through to the great social sin of the Christian conquering genocide against the Original Peoples of the Americas (which still continues today).

That social sin also continued with the torturous and murderous modern Atlantic Slave System, which violently kidnapped tens of millions of African youth, caused the death of millions in the "Middle Passage," and then brutally enslaved tens of millions for hundreds of years. Many Catholic religious orders and Catholic bishops in the Americas themselves oppressively owned and exploited slaves.

---

[4] In the Vatican Palace, tourists visiting the Vatican Museum regularly pass through the "Hall of Constantine." That Hall contains four enormous frescos about Constantine, one of which displays the legend of his "Vision of the Cross." The frescos were commissioned in the 16th Century by Pope Julius. Clearly, Julius still celebrated the Constantinian legacy. (The great Italian painter Raphael began the frescos, but they were reportedly completed by Raphael's disciples after his death.)

The Western form of the Constantinian imperial-episcopal alliance later evolved during the late 19th and early 20th Centuries into Modern Western Industrial Colonialism. Catholic examples of Modern Western Industrial Colonialism included Catholic Belgian King Leopold's personally held "Congo Free State," which caused the unjust killing of millions of people, and the 20th-Century 'imperial' conquest of Ethiopia by the officially 'Catholic' Italian and papally endorsed fascist state of Benito Mussolini.

Predominantly Protestant modern examples included the vast British Empire across Africa, Asia, and the Caribbean, including the genocide inflicted by starvation on Ireland by Britain, as well as the United States' genocidal military attacks on the Original Peoples of the continent, and most infamously in the Cherokee "Trail of Tears." They also included Modern Western Neo-Colonialism throughout Africa, the Asian/Pacific region, and the Latin American/Caribbean region.

Thus, "Cross and sword," and later machine gun, continued in Western partnership into the 20th Century.

4

STAGE 1 – CLERICAL CELIBACY

HIGH-MEDIEVAL LEGISLATION BY

THE GREGORIAN PAPACY

I N 'REFORMING' ZEAL FOR HYPER-MASCULINE TRANSCENDENCE, the papal leaders of the 11th and 12th Century 'Gregorian Reform,' inspired by the rich and powerful Benedictine monastic network of Cluny, set out to impose an extreme Neo-Platonist anti-sexual model on traditionally married Western Catholic bishops and presbyters.

In a cruel attack on the Catholic wives and children of traditionally married Western Catholic bishops and presbyters, as well as on the bishops and presbyters themselves, a pope of the 'Gregorian Reform' even declared clerical marriages to be *"heretical."*

That ridiculous claim became a source of great tension with the Eastern Churches, which rejected such an absurdity that so clearly contradicted the New Testament. That ridiculous also claim aggravated the 11th-Century East-West Schism between the Western and Eastern Churches. In addition, it contributed hundreds of years later to the success of the Protestant Reformation, which rightfully rejected the anti-evangelical imposition of Clerical Celibacy and which so many Northern-European Catholic clerics, often living in forbidden common-law marriages, enthusiastically embraced.

The long historical drive by fanatical Christians to force a monastic-celibate model on traditionally married Western bishops and diocesan presbyters finally triumphed in the so-called Gregorian Reform, named after Pope Gregory VII who was Bishop of Rome in the late 11th Century (1073 to 1085).

Known earlier as Hildebrand and inspired by the Benedictine monasticism of Cluny, Gregory pursued his cruel campaign to force by coercive police-power all Western bishops and presbyters, who had continued the thousand-year old Catholic tradition of episcopal and presbyteral families, *to abandon their Catholic wives and their Catholic children.*[1]

The contemporary historian Anne Llewellyn Barstow, in her scholarly study MARRIED PRIESTS AND THE REFORMING PAPACY,[2] has documented that the monastic-inspired 'Gregorian Reform' not only removed by police-force the wives of bishops and presbyters from their homes, but often forced their wives into *homelessness, prostitution, slavery, and even suicide.* With scholarly understatement, Barstow has described that cruel papal attack on the families of Catholic bishops and presbyters as the *"monasticizing of the clergy."*

Battle between "Gay" & "Straight" Clergy

Further, Anne Llewellyn Barstow and the earlier historian Henry Lea, both distinguished scholars, have stated that written records of resistance by traditionally married bishops and presbyters suggest that there was *a homosexual clerical network* behind the 'reforming' papal attack on clerical families.

---

[1] On this period, see also the classic study by Henry C. Lea, HISTORY OF SACERDOTAL CELIBACY IN THE CHRISTIAN CHURCH (Kessinger Publishing, 2003), with the original published in 1867. Lea, a scholar of the Medieval Church, was at one-time President of the American Historical Society.

[2] Anne Llewellyn Barstow, MARRIED PRIESTS AND THE REFORMING PAPACY: THE 11TH CENTURY DEBATES (Edwin Mellen, 1982).

Further, in his celebrated work CHRISTIANITY, SOCIAL TOLERANCE, AND HOMOSEXUALITY, the late distinguished Yale historian John Boswell documented a medieval clerical tolerance of homosexuality.[3] Yet it was during this same period of "tolerance" that the monastic-inspired papal attack on the Christian marriages and families of Western bishops and presbyters occurred. Why tolerance on one side, but not on the other? In response to that question, Anne Llewellyn Barstow has summarized Boswell's honest narrative:

> *The Gregorian church ... in the century 1050-1150 created no legislation against gay clergy. Indeed, it has been argued that this was a period in which homosexuality flourished among clerics, especially in monasteries, and that since monks gained the ascendency in the church at this time, the legislative centers of the church had little choice but to go light on the question of men who loved men.*

> *John Boswell claims that St. Anselm and several of his pupils, Pope Alexander II and Archbishop Lanfranc, Archbishop Ralph of Tours and his beloved "Flora," Bishop John of Orléans, Bishop William Longchamp of Ely, and most notably Ailred of Rievaulx and his Simon all represent influential churchmen whose actions and/or writings help make this century notable for clerical homosexuality.*

> *Boswell goes so far as to claim that "there was more than a coincidental relation between gay sexuality and some of the [celibacy] reforms ... A satire against a reforming bishop specifically accuses him of hostility to clerical marriage because of his own homosexual disposition." There is some evidence of a power struggle between gay and married clergy over whose predilections would be stigmatized. Indeed, we will see that several [medieval] married clerical authors will express themselves vehemently on just that point.*[4]

---

[3] John Boswell, CHRISTIANITY, SOCIAL TOLERANCE, AND HOMOSEXUALITY: *Gay People in Western Europe from the Beginning of the Christian Era to the Fourteenth Century* (University of Chicago Press, 2005.)

[4] Barstow, MARRIED PRIESTS, pp. 113-114; Boswell, CHRISTIANITY, pp. 210-227.

How sad the apparent medieval battle between "gay" and "straight" clergy. In that case, for the clerical world at least, the "gay" side won, and the non-evangelical legacy of canonically mandatory male Clerical Celibacy became institutionalized in the Latin or Roman Church.

In the wider society and over longer history, however, "straight" prejudice would inflict vicious hatred on "gay" people. Yet all persons on both sides are our loving Creator's beloved children, and all persons on both sides bear the sacred image of the Creator's beauty, dignity, and goodness.

Misogynist Contempt
for Women

A horrendous part of that vicious anti-evangelical campaign was an underlying misogynist contempt for women. Barstow and Lea both pointed to *hate-filled misogynist language* from some leaders of that 'Reform.'

The worst-known examples came from Pietro Damiani (c. 1007-1072), known in English as "Peter Damien." A Benedictine monk, later a cardinal, still later a declared saint, he served as the lead papal agent of the cruel Gregorian attack on the Catholic families of Western bishops and presbyters.

Damiani's vicious words betray a horrendous contempt for women, and in particular for female bodies. As an example, Barstow has cited one of Damiani's "fulminations" against the Catholic women who shared in the apostolic tradition of married bishops and presbyters:

> *I speak to you, o charmers of the clergy, appetizing flesh of the devil, that casting away from paradise, you, poison of the minds, death of souls, companions of the very stuff of sin, the cause of our ruin.*

> *You, I say, I exhort you women of the ancient enemy, you bitches, sows, screech-owls, night owls, she-wolves, blood-suckers ... Come now, hear me, harlots prostitutes, with your lascivious kisses, you wallowing*

places for fat pigs, couches for unclean spirits, demi-goddesses, sirens, witches.

You vipers full of madness, parading the ardor of your ungovernable lust, through your lovers you mutilate Christ, who is the head of the clergy ... you snatch away the unhappy men from their ministry of the sacred altar ... that you may strangle them in the slimy glue of your passion ...

The ancient foe pants to invade the summit of the church's chastity through you ... **They should kill you.**[5] *(Bold font added.)*

In still other "tirades" against the wives of presbyters and bishops, Damiani repeated his hatred for women:

The hands that touch the body and blood of Christ must not have touched the genitals of a whore ... I have attempted to place the restraints of continence upon the genitals of the priesthood, upon those who have the high honor of touching the body and blood of Christ.[6]

Yet Barstow also told a story about how Damiani's own mother, after his birth, had refused to nurse him, and only the intervention of a priest's wife had saved the life of the baby.

As the infant Peter lay withering away, an angel of mercy came from an unexpected and ... ironic source: a neighboring priest's wife took pity on the starving infant and talked his mother into offering him her breast, thereby saving the life of **the future scourge of priestly families.** *(Bold font added.)* [7]

In that misogynist language of that monastic-inspired papal attack on the families of traditionally married Western bishops and presbyters, we see clearly the infection of Western Catholic spirituality by the negative teachings still spreading contamination from certain anti-

---

[5] Cited by Barstow, MARRIED PRIESTS, pp. 60-61.

[6] Cited by Barstow, MARRIED PRIESTS, pp. 59-60.

[7] Barstow, MARRIED PRIESTS, pp. 58-59.

material philosophical schools rooted in late classical Hellenism. Those negative teachings disparaged material creation, the human body, human sexuality, and especially women's bodies.

Wives & Children
Condemned to Slavery

Anne Llewellyn Barstow further pointed out that ecclesiastical decrees, at both papal and regional levels, ordered that *the wives and children of married clerics should be sold into slavery.*[8]

Henry Lea also documented that Pope Leo IX (1049-1054) had ordered *the enslavements of presbyters' wives,* when the couple refused to be separated. Similarly, Lea noted, Pope Urban II (1088-1099) – another imposer of the 'Gregorian Reform,' founder of the modern papal Curia, and launcher of the first medieval military "Crusade" – *ordered 'recalcitrant' clerical wives into slavery.*

Lea also noted that Urban even "offered the wives' servitude as a bribe to the nobles who should aid in thus purifying the Church."[9] Further, the historian Earl Evelyn Sperry, dating the "beginning of a crusade against the married clergy" to 1049 (first year of Leo IX's papacy) and describing the Benedictine monk Pietro Damiani as "principal instigator," pointed out:

> *A council at Rome decreed that the wives of the clergy should be attached as* **slaves to the Lateran Palace***, and bishops of the church were urged to inflict the same punishments upon the wives of priests. (Bold font added.)*

---

[8] Barstow, MARRIED PRIESTS, p. 43. Leo, also a promoter of the power of Cluny, had brought Hildebrand with him to Rome and, according to Lea, dramatically "magnified" the distinction between "clergy and laity." Lea, HISTORY OF SACERDOTAL CELIBACY, p. 154.

[9] Lea, HISTORY OF SACERDOTAL CELIBACY, p. 198.

The Lateran Palace was, of course, the pope's palace. In addition, Sperry reported that later the Hungarian Council of Ofen (1279) enacted that the *children of ecclesiastics should be* the *slaves of the church."* (Italics added.)[10]

Papal Lust for
Theocratic Imperial Power

Ultimately, however, according to Earl Evelyn Sperry, what stood behind the cruel 'Gregorian Reform' was the *monastic-inspired papal lust for theocratic imperial power.* Thus, Sperry wrote:

> *With the election of Hildebrand to the Papal chair ... a celibate clergy was indispensable to a realization of his views concerning the position of the Pope in the affairs of the world. His theories are clearly set forth in the* DICTATUS PAPAE ... *This enunciation of Papal rights ... is tantamount to a declaration that the Pope is the* **autocrat of the church**. *(Bold font added.)*

> *As to the powers of the Pope in secular affairs, Gregory declared that he might depose emperors, that he might annul the decrees of all earthly authorities, but that no one could annul Papal decrees, and that he was to be judged by no one. [According to] the* DICTATUS PAPAE ... **all earthly rulers and powers are amenable and subordinate to the pope**. *(Bold front added.)*[11]

---

[10] For both preceding quotes, see Earl Evelyn Sperry, AN OUTLINE OF THE HISTORY OF CLERICAL CELIBACY IN WESTERN EUROPE TO THE COUNCIL OF TRENT (Doctoral Dissertation for Columbia University, 1905), pp. 41-43. The author had been a University Fellow at Columbia University and later became a professor of history at Syracuse University.

[11] That high-medieval papal claim to global theocratic power later evolved into what is called the "Doctrine of Discovery," which was used to justify the European invasion of the Americas and European-American genocide against the Americas' First Nations. See Steven Newcomb, PAGANS IN THE PROMISED LAND: DECODING THE DOCTRINE OF DISCOVERY, Third Edition (Fulcrum Publishing, 2008). See also Newcomb's essay "Five Hundred Years of Injustice," published by the Indigenous Law Institute at:

Sperry continued:

> As spiritual chief of the world, it was necessary that the Pope should have for his agents **a body of men without local attachments and without personal interests** to which they might sacrifice the welfare of the church. (Bold font added.)

> It was necessary that their powers should be devoted exclusively to defense and aggrandizement of this great ecclesial institution.

> To create a body of men with such singleness of purpose, it was also necessary, besides cutting of all personal interest, to **distinguish them sharply from the people they were to rule.** (Bold font added.)

> The indelible spiritual attributes conferred at ordination accomplished this to some degree, but celibacy was a much more obvious and striking distinction ... [Celibacy would] deprive the clergy of the cares, ambitions and interests which the rearing of a family involves, and it would **isolate them from their fellow men**. (Bold front added.)[12]

Henry Lea, writing earlier, concurred with this analysis:

> Hildebrand ... had conceived **a scheme of hierarchical autocracy** ... To the realization of this ideal he devoted his life with a fiery zeal and unshaken purpose that shrank from no obstacle, and to it he was ready to sacrifice not only the [people] who stood in his path, but also the immutable principles of truth and justice ...

> Such a man could comprehend the full importance of the rule of celibacy, not alone as essential to the ascetic purity of the Church, but as **necessary to the theocratic structure** which he proposed to elevate on the ruins of kingdoms and empires. (Bold front added.)[13]

Thus, papal leaders and their often-monastic agents implemented a misogynist campaign against episcopal and presbyteral families. They

---

http://ili.nativeweb.org/sdrm_art.html.

[12] For these and the preceding paragraphs, Sperry, OUTLINE, pp. 26-27.

[13] Lea, HISTORY, pp. 181-182.

did so in support of the Gregorian lust for theocratic power, supported by a deformed monastic contempt for women.

Meanwhile, baptized Catholic wives of bishops and presbyters, their baptized Catholic children, and their baptized and ordained Catholic husbands and fathers, all became tragic victims of the misogynist and monastic-inspired papal lust for theocratic power.

There were other important issues in the 'Gregorian Reform,' especially the debate over lay-investiture and the papal-imperial struggle. Nonetheless, there is no question about the *deep misogyny,* and there is no question about *the papal lust for theocratic power*.

Finally, there is also no question but that *the so-called 'Gregorian Reform' rejected the apostolic tradition of married bishops and presbyters*, which is affirmed by the New Testament and which continues today, at least for presbyters, within practically all the Eastern Catholic and Eastern Orthodox Churches, as well as within the Western-rooted Protestant Churches.

Even so, the 11th-Century forced imposition of Clerical Celibacy – again, inspired by a fanatical and misogynist distortion of Benedictine Monasticism, and mandated by the Gregorian papacy's lust for theocratic power – constituted the second historical step in the legislation of Clericalism for the Western or Roman Catholic Church.

Yet that step has led, as we now know so well, to the horrendous pathologies of clerical sexual abuse and clerical cover-up. While we always need to remember that such horrendous pathologies can be traced only to a minority of Roman Catholic bishops and presbyters, we also need to remember that it has been the institutional system of Roman Clericalism that enabled such outrageous sins to be committed, covered up, and perpetuated.

Misunderstanding Clerical Celibacy
as a Religious Vow

Despite its non-evangelical legislative origin, mandatory Roman Catholic Clerical Celibacy continues in the West partly because there is a common public misunderstanding that diocesan presbyters in the Roman Catholic Church take a spiritual and voluntary "vow" of celibacy. But that is not the case. Ordained members of Roman Catholic religious orders or congregations do take a voluntary and spiritual "vow" of "chastity," but diocesan candidates for ordination do not.

Instead, diocesan candidates for ordination make a compulsory promise to obey the Canon Law of the Roman Catholic Church, which forbids marriage to its diocesan clergy (apart from the recent exception of married Protestant ministers who convert to Catholicism and wish to become Roman Catholic priests). That acceptance is not a spiritual act, however, but only a legal (canonical) one.

Further, if given a choice, many diocesan candidates for ordination would presumably prefer to follow the Eastern Catholic tradition and become married prior to ordination.[14]

---

[14] Such a choice for marriage would certainly have been the case in earlier decades, before what many judge to be the growth of a large and disproportional percentage of homosexually oriented persons within the Roman Catholic clergy. In wake of the Second Ecumenical Council of the Vatican as well as in the wake of the late-modern "Sexual Revolution," large numbers of heterosexually oriented Roman Catholic presbyters resigned to marry. Across Western Civilization, that large exodus seems to have been followed by a greater percentage of homosexually oriented persons entering Roman Catholic seminaries. Legitimate questions can be asked, therefore, whether there is indeed an unusually large presence of homosexually oriented persons within the late-modern Western Roman Catholic clerical system. If that is true, might it be further aggravating the cultural gulf between the clerical system and the wider Roman Catholic *Laos*, and as a result further weakening the Roman Catholic evangelization in the West? But, apart from such questions about an imbalanced composition in relation to evangelization, it remains important to remember that homosexually oriented seminarians, presbyters, and bishops remain beloved children of God, created in God's own image, and that they bear the same God-given beauty and dignity as heterosexually oriented seminarians, presbyters, and bishops.

In addition, since diocesan bishops are normally first diocesan presbyters, they have also normally made that canonical promise. But, unless bishops are also members of a religious order, they have never made a religious "vow" of celibacy.

Apostolic Tradition Of
Episcopal & Presbyteral Families

The Western or Roman-Catholic non-evangelical claim that the Christian community's ordained leaders must be celibate fundamentally violates the clear teaching of the New Testament, the apostolic tradition, and the broad experience of the Global Catholic Church.

Jesus' first public miracle was for a wedding feast, and he appears to have chosen mostly married individuals as his apostles. Similarly, as mentioned. the episcopal and presbyteral leaders of the Apostolic Church were typically married.

That apostolic tradition continued in the Western, Latin, or Roman Church *for a thousand years of history.* During that period, Western bishops and diocesan presbyters typically were family people, that is, they had wives and children. Thus, family life was the typical background of candidates for ordination. That family nature of Church leadership also constituted an important resource for evangelization.

In addition, and as already noted, after two-thousand years of Christian history, most presbyters in practically all the twenty-three non-Roman and *sui-juris* Eastern Catholic Churches (again, all in full communion with the Catholic Bishop of Rome) are still married to Catholic women and have Catholic children.

Those Eastern-Catholic presbyteral families have constituted important centers of spiritual and intellectual energy within their Eastern Churches, just as rabbinical families have over millennia constituted similar centers of spiritual and intellectual energy for Jewish communities, and just as the families of Protestant ministers have done for Protestant communities over hundreds of years.

Yet, in the Eastern Churches of the Global Catholic Communion, there are a minority of diocesan presbyters who voluntarily chose celibacy and do not marry. They are often called "monastic priests." That name may sound like a euphemism, since they do not belong to monasteries. But it is an appropriate name, since the ancient Greek word *monos* means alone or single.

Further, we clearly find in the New Testament the foundational witness to the apostolic tradition of most bishops and presbyters being married and having children. Thus, the Epistles of First Timothy and Titus both presume that bishops and presbyters overseeing the communities of Jesus' disciples are married and have children.

I TIMOTHY 3:2-5 states:

> *Therefore, a bishop must be irreproachable, **married only once**, temperate, self-controlled, decent, hospitable, able to teach, not a drunkard, not aggressive, but gentle, not contentious, not a lover of money. **He must manage his own household well, keeping his children under control with perfect dignity**; for if a man does not know how to manage his own household, how can he take care of the church of God? (Bold font added.)*

Similarly, TITUS 1:5-7 states:

> *Appoint presbyters in every town, as I directed you, on condition that a man be blameless, **married only once, with believing children** who are not accused of licentiousness or rebellious. For a bishop as God's steward must be blameless, not arrogant, not irritable, not a drunkard, not aggressive, not greedy for sordid gain. (Again, bold font added.)* [15]

---

[15] Note that, in the early church, bishops and presbyters were not yet clearly distinguished.

Having a successful marriage and well-managed children was a typical expectation for ordination in apostolic times and beyond. Certainly, there were exceptions like St. Paul, who never married. But being married and having children was the common situation for bishops and presbyters for the first thousand years of the Western Catholic Church. And it was important for evangelization.

And again, in practically all the Eastern Orthodox Churches and Eastern Catholic Churches, as well as in the Western-rooted Protestant Churches, presbyters or ministers are typically married. Also, their families often play important roles in their Christian communities, as well as in their wider societal communities.

Over against the perhaps hundreds of late-medieval and modern Western Catholic theological volumes defending the 11th-Century papacy's cruel and forced imposition of mandatory Clerical Celibacy on its bishops and diocesan presbyters, the clear teaching of the New Testament and the unbroken practice of the Apostolic Church in the ancient and continuing witness of the Eastern Catholic and Eastern Orthodox Churches (at least for diocesan presbyters), must certainly rank higher.

5

STAGE 3 - CLERICAL SEMINARIES

EARLY-MODERN LEGLISLATION BY
THE COUNCIL OF TRENT

W hile the late-classical Constantinian legislation of the Clerical State and the high-Medieval Gregorian legislation of Clerical Celibacy constituted the first two stages in the historical development of Catholic Clericalism, the third stage emerged with the early-modern Roman Catholic legislation for Clerical Seminaries by the Council of Trent.

Threatening Historical Context

Held in the Northern Italian city of Trent, extending through twenty-five sessions, and spanning eighteen years from 1545 to 1563, the early-modern Council of Trent gathered at a time of major external and internal threats to Western Christendom.

Externally, in 1453 the Eastern Orthodox capital of Constantinople had fallen to the Turkish-Muslim Ottoman offensive – ending the long reign of the Eastern Roman Empire (alternately known as the Byzantine Empire). Then, in 1480-1481, Muslim-Ottoman forces had invaded

Southern Italy in Apulia, as part of a long-term Muslim-Ottoman offensive to conquer Italy.

Internally, there had been war between the Holy Roman Empire, led by the Spanish Hapsburg Emperor Charles V, and the Papal States in alliance with France. Then, in 1527, rioting Imperial troops plundered Rome and left it reeling in turmoil from rape, pillage, and the slaughter of thousands.

Also, and again internally, in 1517 the German Catholic Augustinian monk Martin Luther had posted his now famous ninety-five theses on the door of the Castle Church in Wittenberg. At that time, the event scarcely attracted noticed beyond its local impact. But it eventually became clear that the new Christian rebellion in the North, inaugurated by Luther, was far more than a local or temporary matter. Subsequently, Luther's 1517 posting would be judged by historians to mark the beginning of the great Protestant Reformation.

That broad and deep 16th-Century's emergence of Protestantism began to tear apart Western Christendom – this time in a North-South divide that would prove as devastating as the earlier 11th-Century's East-West divide, which had constituted the first major geographic shattering of Christian unity.

Thus, when Pope Paul III issued his 1542 Bull of Indiction summoning the Council of Trent, the Western or Roman Catholic Church faced world-historical transformations. Seeming to be in both psychological and spiritual agony, Paul wrote in that Bull:

> *We would fain indeed have remedied the evils wherewith the Christian commonweal had been long afflicted, and well-nigh overwhelmed; but we too, as men compassed with infirmity, felt our strength unequal to take upon us so heavy a burthen.*
>
> *For, whereas we saw that peace was needful to free and preserve the commonweal from the many impending dangers, we found all replete*

with enmities and dissensions; and, above all, the (two) princes, to whom God has entrusted well-nigh the whole direction of events, at enmity with each other.

Whereas we deemed it necessary that there should be one fold and one shepherd, for the Lord's flock in order to maintain the Christian religion in its integrity, and to confirm within us the hope of heavenly things; the unity of the Christian name was rent and well-nigh torn asunder by schisms, dissensions, heresies.

Whereas we could have wished to see the commonwealth safe and guarded against the arms and insidious designs of the Infidels, yet, through our transgressions and the guilt of us all,--the wrath of God assuredly hanging over our sins, – Rhodes had been lost; Hungary ravaged; war both by land and sea had been contemplated and planned against Italy, Austria, and Illyria; whilst our impious and ruthless enemy the Turk was never at rest, and looked upon our mutual enmities and dissensions as his fitting opportunity for carrying out his designs with success.[1]

Such tumultuous events were the social equivalent of a geological earthquake for the West. They revealed that the long medieval period had ended, and that there was emerging the new, though not yet fully developed, "Modern World."

Yet, even though the 16th-Century Council Trent was called to address many threats, the one purpose that would come to define it, and to define Western Catholicism for the next four-hundred years, was the ecclesial construction of the modern Catholic "Counter-Reformation" years, which lasted until the 20th-Century's Second Ecumenical Council of the Vatican.

---

[1] J. Waterworth, Editor & Translator, THE CANONS AND DECREES OF THE SACRED AND OECUMENICAL COUNCIL OF TRENT (London: Dolman, 1848), pp 1-2; available online at: *https://history.hanover.edu/texts/trent/ct23.html.*

Trent's Mandate for
the Modern Seminary System

In terms of the Counter-Reformation, one of most important acts of the Council came from its Twenty-Third Session. In Chapter XVIII of its Decree on the Sacrament of Order (by far, the longest chapter in that Decree), the Council mandated "Seminaries for Clerics."

DECREE ON REFORMATION
CHAPTER XVIII.

Method of establishing Seminaries for Clerics,
and of educating the same therein.

Whereas the age of youth, unless it be rightly trained, is prone to follow after the pleasures of the world; and unless it be formed, from its tender years, unto piety and religion, before habits of vice have taken possession of the whole man, it never will perfectly, and without the greatest, and well-nigh special, help of Almighty God, persevere in ecclesiastical discipline; the holy Synod ordains, that all cathedral, metropolitan, and other churches greater than these, shall be bound, each according to its means and the extent of the diocese, to maintain, to educate religiously, and to train in ecclesiastical discipline, a certain number of youths of their city and diocese, or, if that number cannot be met with there, of that province, in a college to be chosen by the bishop for this purpose near the said churches, or in some other suitable place.

Into this college shall be received such as are at least twelve years old, born in lawful wedlock, and who know how to read and write competently, and whose character and inclination afford a hope that they will always serve in the ecclesiastical ministry. And It wishes that the children of the poor be principally selected; though It does not however exclude those of the more wealthy, provided they be maintained at their own expense, and manifest a desire of serving God and the Church.

The bishop, having divided these youths into as many classes as he shall think fit, according to their number, age, and progress in ecclesiastical discipline, shall, when it seems to him expedient, assign some of them to the ministry of the churches, the others he shall keep in the college to be instructed; and shall supply the place of those who have been withdrawn, by others; that so this college may be a perpetual seminary of ministers of God.

And that the youths may be the more advantageously trained in the aforesaid ecclesiastical discipline, they shall always at once wear the tonsure and the clerical dress; they shall learn grammar, singing, ecclesiastical computation, and the other liberal arts; they shall be instructed in sacred Scripture; ecclesiastical works; the homilies of the saints; the manner of administering the sacraments, especially those things which shall seem adapted to enable them to hear confessions; and the forms of the rites and ceremonies.

The bishop shall take care that they be present every day at the sacrifice of the mass, and that they confess their sins at least once a month; and receive the body of our Lord Jesus Christ as the judgment of their confessor shall direct; and on festivals serve in the cathedral and other churches of the place.[2]

Though there had long been established Catholic cathedral schools and Catholic universities, they had not been exclusively for clerics. Yet Trent mandated a new Catholic educational system exclusively for clerics, apart from the laity and insulated from the wider society. Reflecting on that early-modern innovation (and in the still-surviving

---

[2] The full Chapter XVIII is much longer and runs several more pages. See Waterworth, CANONS AND DECREES, available at: *https://history.hanover.edu/texts/trent/ct23ref2.html.*

Counter-Reformation style), the 2007-2014 Catholic Encyclopedia, in its article titled "Ecclesiastical Seminary," recounts the following:

> *This system of seminary education, which has now become an essential feature of the Church's life, had its origin only in the sixteenth century in a decree of the Council of Trent. Since Christ's mission on earth is to be continued chiefly through diocesan priests, the Apostles and the early popes gave special care to the selection and training of clergy ... But though the training of the clergy was ever held to be a matter of vital importance, we should look in vain during the first centuries for an organized system of clerical education.*[3]

Note the text's erroneous extension the category of "clergy" back into the apostolic period and the early centuries of Christianity.

Intensified Monasticizing of the Diocesan Clergy

Though the Catholic Encyclopedia article does not mention it, the Tridentine ecclesiastical seminary was *an institution modeled on monasticism* (just as the early Gregorian legislation of Clerical Celibacy had drawn on the monastic model). To support that monasticizing of the diocesan clergy, semi-monastic Roman Catholic male religious orders were frequently given responsibility for Roman Catholic seminaries (particularly Sulpicians and Vincentians), in order to form seminarians in a monastic spirituality.

Thus, while in the 11th Century the Gregorian legislation had imposed monastic-like Clerical Celibacy on traditionally married diocesan bishops and presbyters, the 16th Century Tridentine legislation mandated that clerics preparing for ordination were to receive their education within a monastic-like environment (quite different from the environment of their future pastoral ministry).

---

[3] *http://www.newadvent.org/cathen/12694a.htm*

Note again that, until 1972 when there was a revision of Roman Catholic Canon Law, Roman Catholic "seminarians" (students in seminaries) became canonically members of the Clerical State by being initiated into it through the ritual known as "tonsure," which entails cutting part of the candidate's hair.

That ritual, a token-symbol of the traditional monastic tonsure, also revealed the monastic influence on Roman Catholic Clericalism that had begun during the high-medieval period when Benedictine monks were ordained as "priests" (not the typical prior monastic practice), and they were also admitted to the Clerical State.

That sacerdotalization and clericalization of high-medieval Benedictine monasticism also led to a theological distortion of the "priesthood" as if it were something autonomous from the *Laos*, and as not even requiring the presence of another Christian. Thus, Western monastic priests, and later even diocesan priests, began to "say" "private masses" and on a daily basis, with no one present but themselves.

Further, the enormous wealth of high-medieval Benedictine monasticism, particularly the rich and powerful monastic network of Cluny, led to the cultivation of expensive gold-embroidered vestments and jewel-encrusted gold and silver chalices for eucharistic liturgies – quite different from the simple clothing and simple cups at Jesus' Last Supper.

Thus, extension of the ritual of the monastic tonsure to diocesan seminarians, like the earlier imposition of monastic-like Clerical Celibacy on Western bishops and presbyters, further intensified the misunderstanding of the Roman Catholic diocesan "clergy" as a monastic-like male-celibate spiritual caste.

Multiple Segregations of Seminarians

The early-modern Tridentine Clerical Seminary segregated Roman Catholic clerical seminarians in multiple ways.

First, the later development of philosophical and theological disciples within Tridentine seminary education became *intellectually segregated* from the broader intellectual life of the modern Western university, with its ongoing intellectual developments in the study of literature, history, and the natural and human sciences.

That intellectual segregation thus isolated the modern form of Clericalism into a narrow intellectual subculture that became increasingly separated from the of intellectual life of the wider society.

In particular, the Tridentine seminary's teaching of philosophy, eventually based on a modern revival and adaptation of Aristotelian Thomism, failed to sustain a serious intellectual conversation with the wider currents of modern Western philosophy. As a result, a vast intellectual gulf developed between Catholic Neo-Thomism and modern Western philosophy.

That intellectual segregation led to intellectual marginalization of the Catholic intellectual tradition from the wider modern secular intellectual development of Western Civilization. It may even have enabled (at least partially by its absence) the late-modern nihilistic direction now found across much of late-modern Western philosophy, literature, and social science.

Second, the long years of monastic-like seminary formation in the Tridentine seminary also trained Roman Catholic clerical candidates for ordination to live in *spiritual segregation* from the wider Roman Catholic lay community. The seminary experience deliberately fostered a clerical subculture insulated and isolated from the life of the wider *Laos* of Jesus' disciples.

Later, during the late-20th-Century, with the restorationist backlash that arose in reaction to the Second Ecumenical Council of the Vatican, so-called 'conservative' clerical sectors of the modern Tridentine seminary system became part of an even more isolated subculture.

That late-modern Roman Catholic 'conservative' subculture promoted an authoritarian and sometimes arrogant intensification of Tridentine Roman Catholic Clericalism. But that authoritarian form of Clericalism has been recently humbled by the early 21st-Century media disclosure of pervasive Roman Catholic clerical scandals from sexual (and financial) abuse and cover-up.

Third, and most importantly, the long-years of monastic-like formation in an all-male clerical environment further aggravated the Roman Catholic institution of Clericalism's *sexual segregation from women*. Also, that sexual segregation intensified modern Roman Catholic Clericalism's "hyper-masculine" character.[4]

Now, following the recent public exposure of Roman Catholic episcopal and presbyteral scandals of sexual (and financial) abuse and coverup, the hyper-masculine "*clerical-celibate-seminary*" model for the Roman Catholic institution of Clericalism is dramatically alienating women, who make up half of the human race.

*   *   *

We have now reviewed the three historical stages of in the legislative construction of the ecclesial institution known as Roman Catholic Clericalism. Again, they are: 1) late-classical imperial legislation of the Constantinian Clerical State; 2) high-medieval papal legislation of Gregorian Clerical Celibacy; and 3) early-modern conciliar legislation of the Tridentine Clerical Seminary.

---

[4] For more on this theme of hyper-masculinism in the wider modern bourgeois culture, see my earlier-mentioned book, POSTMODERN ECOLOGICAL SPIRITUALITY.

But, within the wider societal crises of the late-modern form of Western Civilization, the three-stage legislative construction of the institution of Roman Catholic Clericalism – as the core strategic institution of the Western Catholic Church – is now breaking down. Within that breakdown, the entrenched institution of Roman Catholic Clericalism has become not only non-evangelical but now also *anti-evangelical*. It is undermining the Western Catholic evangelization.[5]

That breakdown and undermining leaves us with the strategic question: "What is to be done." For an exploration of that question, let us now turn to the Conclusion of this small book.

[5] For further reflections on the seminary aspect of this breakdown, see the essay by Alberto Melloni, "*La messa è finita. Così dopo cinque secoli tramonta la figura del prete*," LA REPUBLICA (Italy), 2017-03-22, available at: *http://ilsismografo.blogspot.it/2017/03/italia-la-messa-e-finita.html*. For an excellent English-language article on this essay see Robert Mickens, "Letter from Rome: The Church's Seminary Problem," COMMONWEAL MAGAZINE, 2017-03-27, available at: *https://www.commonwealmagazine.org/letter-rome-117*. In addition, see Massimo Faggioli, "Trent's long shadow: The abuse crisis and seminaries, dioceses, and the Laity," LA CROIX INTERNATIONAL, at *https://international.la-croix/news/trents-long-shado/8295*, and "Inverting the course: clericalism, centralization, and church reform, LA CROIX INTERNATIONAL, at *https://international.la-croix/ news/inverting-the-course-clericalism-centralization-and-church-reform/8378*.

CONCLUSION

WHAT IS TO BE DONE?

Again, in the late-modern period, the Western "*clerical-celibate-seminary*" model for Roman Catholic presbyters and bishops is breaking down within the 'advanced' industrial countries of Western Civilization. That breakdown is revealed by the dramatic rise in the medium age of Western Roman Catholic presbyters and by the dramatic "shortage of clerical vocations," as well as by the often intellectually weak and sometimes emotionally unhealthy quality of many Western Roman Catholic seminarians.

Breakdown of the
Modern Western Roman Catholic Evangelization

Yet most contemporary Western Roman Catholic bishops, who presumably are good people deeply devoted to the Gospel of Jesus and to God's holy and chosen *Laos*, nonetheless still do not appear to understand the historical breakdown of the modern "*clerical-celibate-seminary*" model of the Western Catholic presbyterate and episcopacy. They also appear still not to understand the relationship of that breakdown to the institution of Roman Catholic Clericalism to the wider historical breakdown of the modern Roman Catholic evangelization across Western Civilization.

During the 19th Century, at the end of the Ancien Régime, most European Roman Catholic bishops remained imprisoned in what we may call their "*aristocratic captivity*." They failed to understand the deep spiritual challenges from the emerging bourgeois political economy of the *Modern Industrial Revolution*. In major regions of Western Europe, that caused the massive failure of evangelization now known as the "loss of the working class."

Today, across the industrial-center countries of Western Civilization, and perhaps especially in the English-speaking countries, we see what we might call the "*bourgeois captivity*" of many Western Roman Catholic bishops. Often enmeshed in a corporate-capitalist model of management and networking, too many Western Catholic bishops seem unable to understand the deep historical-spiritual challenges now emerging from the *Postmodern Electronic Revolution*.[1]

As a result, *another great Western Catholic de-evangelization is now underway*, and this time especially across the 'advanced' English-speaking countries of Western Civilization.

Yet there is no shortage of "vocations" for ordained ministerial leadership within the Protestant Reformation's Evangelical and Pentecostal Churches.[2] The reason is that those still growing Christian movements

---

[1] On the correlation of the breakdown of modern Western Catholic spirituality and the modern Western Catholic evangelization with the contextual breakdown of the entire modern form of Western Civilization, see again my earlier mentioned book, POSTMODERN ECOLOGICAL SPIRITUALITY. According to that study, the Western Catholic breakdowns form part of the wider and correlative Western breakdowns of Modern Psychological Spirituality and Modern Industrial Civilization.

[2] These churches are different from the "mainline" Protestant denominations, which constructed a deracinated academic professionalism for ministerial leadership. Further, the "mainlines" by and large became culturally accommodated to Modernity, and thus often lack the counter-cultural spiritual energy found in the Evangelical and Pentecostal movements. Further, the "mainline" Protestant churches, at least in the United States, have a reverse problem from the Western Roman Catholic one. While they do not have a shortage of "vocations" for pastoral ministry, they often have a shortage of congregations to serve.

have long rejected for ministerial leadership the non-evangelical model of Clericalism, as well as the non-evangelical requirement of celibacy. In their place, *they have long embraced the original lay form of ecclesial leadership*. In addition, many of those pastoral leaders have often embraced the Electronic Revolution as a central medium for evangelization.

More importantly, the globally expanding Evangelical and Pentecostal movements have returned to the ancient Christian tradition of pursuing evangelization, and of discerning ecclesial leadership within evangelization, primarily through locally-rooted lay kinship and friendship networks. In that return, Evangelical and Pentecostal movements frequently ordain local grass-roots leaders, and then often allow them to remain and minister within their local communities – as happened in the original lay movement of Jesus' disciples.[3]

Again, those contemporary Reformation movements have rejected the deracinated and segregated Roman Catholic *"clerical-celibate-seminary"* model for ordained leadership developed in the late-classical, medieval, and modern periods. They have also often rejected the deracinated clerical-professional model developed for the "mainline" Protestant Churches, which have typically sought cultural integration with secular modernization.

Consequently, across the globe, Evangelical and Pentecostal movements, and especially Pentecostal movements which empower women, have been dramatically expanding their evangelization. Of course, such movements have often brought theological problems, like the so-called "Gospel of Prosperity."

---

[3] In the past, I was privileged to teach in two Protestant interdenominational seminaries that reached out especially to Evangelical and Pentecostal pastors and provided them with ongoing graduate-level education, including at the doctoral level. They were New York Theological Seminary in New York City, and its southern offshoot the Florida Center for Theological Studies. Thanks to those experiences, I became deeply impressed by the devoted character of the Evangelical and Pentecostal pastors whom I taught. By the way, in my classes, those pastors became fascinated with Catholic theology and with Catholic Social Teaching.

But, meanwhile within the 'advanced' industrial-center countries, the deracinated and segregated "*clerical-celibate-seminary*" model of the Roman Catholic institution of Clericalism collapses into ever deeper crisis, and sometimes in a pathological and even criminal manner.

That late-modern crisis of the Roman Catholic institution of Clericalism within the industrial center-countries remains inseparable from the Western Roman Catholic Church's non-evangelical law of Clerical Celibacy" for diocesan presbyters and bishops. Changing that papal law will not of itself resolve the late-modern crisis of the Western Roman Catholic evangelization. But it is surely a necessary pre-condition for resolving it.

To address the late-modern breakdown of the institution of Clericalism at the deep cultural-spiritual level, there will also need to be a profound transformation in the Roman Catholic Church's grounding spirituality, as well as a return to the apostolic model of ordaining to the presbyterate local grass-roots lay leaders, who will typically be married – and thus doing so without the Clerical State, without Clerical Celibacy, and without the Clerical Seminary.

Of course, voluntary evangelical celibacy constitutes an important spiritual charism for those whom the Holy Spirit calls to it. But human-made ecclesial law cannot forcibly impose the Holy Spirit's gift of a special charism on an institutional office. When that happens, there occurs an anti-spiritual distortion of the nature of that office, as well as an institutional undermining of its spiritual power.

Further, my larger book POSTMODERN ECOLOGICAL SPIRITUALITY has argued that the postmodern cultural-spiritual transformation, in its deep mythic-symbolic foundation, needs to move beyond both classical hierarchical patriarchy and modern hyper-masculinism (with both carrying undertows of misogyny), toward an egalitarian and co-creative partnership of feminine and masculine historical-spiritual energy.

64

For that reason, across global Catholic Christianity, it is now essential to create regenerative postmodern paths that welcome and support women's spiritual and pastoral gifts

Clericalism as an Institutional Obstacle
to the New Evangelization

As we have seen, since today across most of Western Civilization there is no longer a close alliance between church and state, all three dimensions of the institution of Roman Catholic Clericalism – the late-classical Constantinian Clerical State, high-medieval Gregorian Clerical Celibacy, and the early-modern Tridentine Clerical Seminary – have all become institutional obstacles to the Holy Spirit's call for a postmodern "New Evangelization."

In Europe, across the Americas, and elsewhere as well, Roman Catholics are flooding out of so many clericalized, bureaucratized, and stagnant Western Catholic ecclesial communities into more nurturing and dynamic de-clericalized Evangelical and Pentecostal ecclesial communities (and sometimes into Orthodox ecclesial communities).

As noted, in those expanding Evangelical and Pentecostal communities, their devoted pastors long ago returned to the original apostolic model of *lay ecclesial servant-leadership*. As a result, such pastors in general relate much more effectively to the lay human experiences and lay spiritual needs of the wider *Laos* that they serve. And their families typically amplify their pastoral power.

Yet, as we have also seen, from the perspective of Catholic theology, there are often serious problems with many aspects of Evangelical and Pentecostal theologies, including biblical literalism, an anti-incarnational intoxication with violent apocalypticism, and the so-called "Gospel of Prosperity," all of which sometimes combine with theological support for political authoritarianism and for endless war.

But serious as those theological problems may be, they are distinct from the Evangelical and Pentecostal form of pastoral servant-leadership that has returned to the apostolic lay paradigm. Further, I believe that what explains the global growth of these Evangelical and Pentecostal communities is not their often-problematic theologies, but rather *the lay nature of their pastoral servant-leadership, which is the same model given to is by Jesus and the New Testament.*

Seeking a De-Clericalized & Authentically Postmodern Church

For that reason, the Western or Roman Catholic Church, in order to seek an authentically postmodern New Evangelization, now needs to deconstruct its three-part institutional system of clerical uprooting and segregation from the wider holy *Laos*. Only when that happens will the Sacrament of Orders in the Western Roman Catholic Church become re-laicized, and only then will it become liberated for evangelical re-empowerment according to its apostolic origins.

Thus, for the Roman Catholic Church, *a de-clericalized regeneration of the Sacrament of Orders* – along with a correlative reawakening of the wider and holy Catholic *Laos* to its evangelical identity and mission – constitutes a *sine qua non* for fully opening Roman Catholic evangelization within the emerging Postmodern Era to the life-giving power of the Holy Spirit.

In addition, despite what some have claimed, de-clericalization today would not constitute secularizing de-sacralization. Rather, it would constitute a sacral return to the New Testament's definition of the entire People of God – including both its servant-leaders and all its other members – as forming together the holy *Laos*, which is also the priestly *Kleros*.

Yet again, as mentioned earlier, deconstruction of the three-stage legislative construction of the Roman Catholic institution of Clericalism

66

would have to be done gradually and with the prudence of practical wisdom.

Further, that deconstruction would have to occur with the support of *an authentically postmodern global Catholic renaissance*, which needs to be at once artistic, intellectual, and canonical, and which needs to lead to a truly global and ecumenical council of all twenty-four Catholic Churches within the Global Catholic Communion.

Lastly, it would have to occur within the context of what I have elsewhere described as *the symbolic-mythic transition from Modern Psychological Spirituality to Postmodern Ecological Spirituality*.

All that is a great deal to accomplish, but it is what needs to be done. There is no other route. And the Holy Spirit will show the way – provided we become open to her prophetic and mystical inspirations.

APPENDIX

"GET RID OF THE CLERGY,

BUT KEEP HOLY ORDERS"

*The following article was published
in Commonweal Magazine on 13 April 2018.
It is reprinted here with permission.*

I n their fascinating exchange on the clergy ("Imagine There's No Clergy"), William M. Shea and David Cloutier seem unable to distinguish the "Clerical State" from the "Sacrament of Orders." One author appears to seek elimination of both for the sake of evangelical renewal, while the other appears to seek preservation of both for the same reason.

Contrary to what appears to be the argument of both authors, the Sacrament of Orders and the Clerical State are historically distinct and institutionally separable. During its first three centuries, the Greek-speaking church developed and sustained the Sacrament of Orders for *episcopoi, presbyteroi,* and *diaconoi* (bishops, presbyters, and deacons). But there was as yet no Clerical State. That came only in the fourth century, through the Constantinian fusion of the Catholic Church with the Roman Imperial State.

In that fusion, the leadership of the Roman Empire transferred imperial "hierarchical" privileges from the pagan priesthood to the ordained servant-leaders of the Catholic Church. The new imperial "clergy" were legally empowered to rule over the non-clerical "laity." Prior to this development, the entire church (meaning both ordained servant-leaders and the entire membership) had been understood as both sacredly lay (the holy *laos*) and as divinely chosen (the holy *kleros*).

Since the Sacrament of Orders and the Clerical State are historically distinct, the former having existed for three centuries without the latter, that means they are also institutionally separable. Indeed, the Canon Law of the Western or Roman Catholic Church recognizes the distinction between the Sacrament of Orders and the Clerical State. When Roman Catholic "priests" decide to marry, they may apply for a *"reduction to the lay state."* This 'reduction' removes them from the Clerical State but, according to official teaching, they "ontologically" remain ordained "priests."

Today, across the Americas and elsewhere, Western Catholics are flooding out of often stagnant Catholic parishes into more dynamic Evangelical and Pentecostal congregations

In short, the Sacrament of Orders is of apostolic origin, while the Clerical State is a fourth-century legal construction by the Roman Empire. Later, in the eleventh century, the Western Catholic clergy were further segregated from the laity when the papacy imposed mandatory celibacy on all diocesan presbyters and bishops in the West. (By so doing, the papacy also forced many wives of bishops and presbyters into homelessness, slavery, or even suicide. See Anne Llewellyn Barstow's book *Married Priests and the Reforming Papacy*.)

Then, in the sixteenth century, the Council of Trent segregated the clergy still more by mandating formation in monastery-like Clerical Seminaries. These structures uprooted candidates for ordination from their original lay communities of kinship and friendship, prepared them to become part of a "chosen" clerical caste, and molded them for work as interchangeable parts within a standardized and often-impersonal ecclesiastical bureaucracy.

Today, across the Americas and elsewhere, Western Catholics are flooding out of often stagnant Catholic parishes into more dynamic Evangelical and Pentecostal congregations, whose pastors long ago returned to the original apostolic model of non-clerical and lay servant-leadership. In general, these lay pastors relate much more effectively to the lay experiences and spiritual needs of the wider *Laos* that they serve.

Of course, from a Catholic perspective, these churches also suffer from serious theological problems, including biblical literalism and the so-called "Gospel of Prosperity." And all too often these churches support patriarchy and authoritarian governments. But the Catholic Church can still learn from their non-clerical model of pastoral ministry, with its clear roots in the presbyterate of the early church.

https://www.commonwealmagazine.org/get-rid-clergy

ABOUT THE AUTHOR

 JOE HOLLAND, an eco-philosopher and Catholic theologian, explores the global transition to a democratic and regenerative Postmodern Ecological Civilization.

Joe completed his Ph.D. from the University of Chicago in the field of Ethics & Society, which was an interdisciplinary dialogue of Theology with Philosophy and Social Science. At Chicago, he studied Theology with David Tracy, Philosophy with Paul Ricoeur, and Social Science with Gibson Winter. He was also a Fulbright Scholar in Philosophy at the Universidad Católica in Santiago, Chile during the last year of the democratic-socialist government of President Salvador Allende, which was overthrown by the murderous dictatorship of General Augusto Pinochet.

Joe is Emeritus Professor of Philosophy & Religion at Saint Thomas University in Miami Gardens, Florida, and a still active Adjunct Professor in its School of Law; Permanent Visiting Professor at the Universidad Nacional del Altiplano in Puno, Peru; President of Pax Romana / Catholic Movement for Intellectual & Cultural Affairs USA, and Editor of its Pacem in Terris Press, with both based in Washington DC; Vice-Chair of Catholic Scholars for Worker Justice, with offices in in Boston, Massachusetts; and a member of the International Association for Catholic Social Thought, based at the Catholic University of Leuven in Belgium.

Earlier, Joe served for 15 years as Research Associate at the Washington DC Center of Concern, created jointly by the international Jesuits and the US Catholic Bishops to work with the United Nations on global issues. Later, he taught at New York Theological Seminary in New York City, at the Theological School of Drew University in Madison, New Jersey, and at the Florida Center for Theological Studies in Miami, Florida.

In addition, for both the Center of Concern and Pax Romana, he served as NGO Representative to the Economic and Social Council of the United Nations in New York City.

Joe also served as Research Coordinator for the 1976 Theology in the Americas Conference. Later, he co-founded the American Catholic Lay Network, the National Conference on Religion & Labor (co-sponsored by the AFL-CIO), and Catholic Scholars for Worker Justice. Plus, he was founding Director of the Pallottine Institute for Lay Leadership & Research at Seton Hall University.

Joe has published 17 other books and many articles. His book with Peter Henriot, *Social Analysis: Linking Faith and Justice*, has more than 100,000 copies in print, including 2 US editions, 5 foreign-language editions, and 2 foreign English editions. He was also consultant-writer for the 1975 document *This Land is Home to Me* (A Pastoral Letter on Powerlessness in Appalachia by the Catholic Bishops of the Region), and for its 1995 sequel document *At Home in the Web of Life* (A Pastoral Message from the Catholic Bishops of Appalachia on Sustainable Communities).

In the United States, Joe has lectured at Georgetown, Harvard, Notre Dame, Princeton, and many other universities. Internationally, he has lectured at Institut Catholique in Paris, France; Sophia University in Tokyo, Japan; Pontifical Catholic University in São Paulo, Brazil; Pontifical Catholic University in Porto Alegre, Brazil; Universidad Mayor de San Andres in La Paz, Bolivia; and Universidad Nacional del Altiplano in Puno, Peru.

In 1986, Joe received the Boston Paulist Center's Isaac Hecker Award for Social Justice; in 2002, the Athena Medal of Excellence from the Universidad Nacional del Altiplano in Peru; and in 2013 an Irish Echo Award for contribution to the US labor movement.

Joe is married to Paquita Biascoechea-Martinez Holland, a native of Puerto Rico, and they have two wonderful grown children and four wonderful young grandchildren. His too infrequent hobby is sailing, especially in the beautiful green waters of the Caribbean Sea.

OTHER BOOKS
FROM PACEM IN TERRIS PRESS

BRETTON WOODS INSTITUTIONS & NEOLIBERALISM
Historical Critique of Policies, Structures, & Governance
of the International Monetary Fund & the World Bank, with Case Studies
Mark J. Wolff, 2018

SAINT JOHN OF THE CROSS
His Prophetic Mysticism in the Historical Context of Sixteenth-Century Spain
Cristóbal Serrán-Pagán y Fuentes. 2018

PADRE MIGUEL
A Memoir of My Catholic Missionary Experience in Bolivia
amidst Postcolonial Transformation of Church and State
Michael J. Gillgannon, 2018

POSTMODERN ECOLOGICAL SPIRITUALITY
Catholic-Christian Hope for the Dawn of a Postmodern Ecological Civilization Rising
from within the Spiritual Dark Night of Modern Industrial Civilization
Joe Holland, 2017

JOURNEYS TO RENEWED CONSECRATION
Religious Life after Fifty Years of Vatican II
Emeka Obiezu, OSA & John Szura, OSA, Editors, 2017

THE CRUEL ELEVENTH-CENTURY IMPOSITION OF
WESTERN CLERICAL CELIBACY
A Monastic-Inspired Attack on Catholic Episcopal & Clerical Families
Joe Holland, 2017

LIGHT, TRUTH, & NATURE
Practical Reflections on Vedic Wisdom & Heart-Centered Meditation
In Seeking a Spiritual Basis for Nature, Science, Evolution, & Ourselves
Thomas Pliske, 2017

THOMAS BERRY IN ITALY
Reflections on Spirituality & Sustainability
Elisabeth M. Ferrero, Editor, 2016

PETER MAURIN'S
ECOLOGICAL LAY NEW MONASTICISM
A Catholic Green Revolution Developing
Rural Ecovillages, Urban Houses of Hospitality,
& Eco-Universities for a New Civilization
Joe Holland, 2015

PROTECTION OF RELIGIOUS MINORITIES
A Symposium Organized by Pax Romana at the United Nations
and the United Nations Alliance of Civilizations
Dean Elizabeth F. Defeis & Peter F. O'Connor, Editors, 2015

BOTTOM ELEPHANTS
Catholic Sexual Ethics & Pastoral Practice in Africa:
The Challenge of Women Living within Patriarchy
& Threatened by HIV-Positive Husbands
Daniel Ude Asue, 2014

CATHOLIC LABOR PRIESTS
Five Giants in the United States Catholic Bishops Social Action Department
Volume I of US Labor Priests During the 20th Century
Patrick Sullivan, 2014

CATHOLIC SOCIAL TEACHING & UNIONS
IN CATHOLIC PRIMARY & SECONDARY SCHOOLS
The Clash between Theory & Practice within the United States
Walter "Bob" Baker, 2014

SPIRITUAL PATHS TO
A GLOBAL & ECOLOGICAL CIVILIZATION
Reading the Signs of the Times with Buddhists, Christians, & Muslims
John Raymaker & Gerald Grudzen, with Joe Holland, 2013

PACEM IN TERRIS
Its Continuing Relevance for the Twenty-First Century
(Papers from the 50th Anniversary Conference at the United Nations)
Josef Klee & Francis Dubois, Editors, 2013

PACEM IN TERRIS
Summary & Commentary for the Famous Encyclical Letter
of Pope John XXIII on World Peace
Joe Holland, 2012

100 YEARS OF CATHOLIC SOCIAL TEACHING
DEFENDING WORKERS & THEIR UNIONS
Summaries & Commentaries for Five Landmark Papal Encyclicals
Joe Holland, 2012

HUMANITY'S AFRICAN ROOTS
Remembering the Ancestors' Wisdom
Joe Holland, 2012

THE "POISONED SPRING" OF ECONOMIC LIBERTARIANISM
Menger, Mises, Hayek, Rothbard: A Critique from
Catholic Social Teaching of the Austrian School of Economics
Pax Romana / Cmica-usa
Angus Sibley, 2011

BEYOND THE DEATH PENALTY
The Development in Catholic Social Teaching
Florida Council of Catholic Scholarship
D. Michael McCarron & Joe Holland, Editors, 2007

THE NEW DIALOGUE OF CIVILIZATIONS
A Contribution from Pax Romana
International Catholic Movement for Intellectual & Cultural Affairs
Pax Romana / Cmica-usa
Roza Pati & Joe Holland, Editors, 2002

OTHER BOOKS BY JOE HOLLAND

In Addition to his earlier listed books published by Pacem in Terris Press

---

MODERN CATHOLIC SOCIAL TEACHING 1740-1958
The Popes Confront the Industrial Age
Paulist Press, 2003

"THE EARTH CHARTER"
A Study Book of Reflection for Action
Co-Author Elisabeth Ferrero
Redwoods Press, 2002
(Also available in Italian & Portuguese versions)

VARIETIES OF POSTMODERN THEOLOGY
Co-Editors David Griffin & William Beardslee,
State University of New York Press, 1989

CREATIVE COMMUNION
Toward a Spirituality of Work
Paulist Press, 1989

AMERICAN AND CATHOLIC
The New Debate
Co-Editor Anne Barsanti
Pillar Books, 1988

VOCATION AND MISSION OF THE LAITY
Co-Author Robert Maxwell
Pillar Books, 1986

SOCIAL ANALYSIS
Linking Faith and Justice
Co-Author Peter J. Henriot SJ
Orbis Books, 1980 & 1983
(Also available in multiple languages)

THE AMERICAN JOURNEY
A Theology in the Americas Working Paper
IDOC, 1976

The preceding books are available at:

www.amazon.com/books

Made in the USA
Columbia, SC
21 February 2021